IBRAHITT

what does
Islām
Say ?

Abortion . Adoption . AIDS . Animal welfare .
Calender . Capital Punishment . Contraception .
Crescent . Divorce . Drugs & Alcohol .
Environment . Festivals . Food & Drinks .
Homosexuality . Jihād . Marriage . Music . Muslim
Schools . Parents & Children . Racism . Slavery .
Suicide . Surrogacy . Women

The Muslim Educational Trust

Copyright:
THE MUSLIM EDUCATIONAL TRUST 1425 AH / 2004 CE

1st Edition	March 1993
	Reprinted July 1993
	Reprinted October 1995
2nd Edition	January 1997
3rd Edition	June 1998
4th Edition	April 2004

British Library Cataloguing-in-Publication Data
A catalogue record of this book is available from the British Library

Published by:
The Muslim Educational Trust
130 Stroud Green Road
London N4 3RZ
UK
Tel: 020 7272 8502
Fax: 020 7281 3457
URL: www.muslim-ed-trust.org.uk

Email: info@muslim-ed-trust.org.uk

ISBN 0 907261 42 6
Printed and bound in Great Britain by:
Hobbs The Printer.
Brunel Road
Totton, Hampshire
SO40 3WX
Tel: 023 8066 4800 Fax 023 8066 4801 http://www.hobbs.co.uk

Contents

Foreword

In the Name of Allāh, the Most Merciful, the Most Kind

The *Muslim Educational Trust (MET)*, the UK's oldest Muslim educational organisation (established in 1966), regularly receives queries from schools, students, teachers, educational institutions and bodies, and those interested in the many aspects of Islām, a religion with over 1.3 billion adherents worldwide, and the fastest growing of the major faiths.

The response to many of these queries is to send a fact sheet on one of a wide range of topics, including: abortion, Aids, drug abuse, suicide, surrogacy, mosques, marriage, music and the status of women, etc. Readers should note that these responses are necessarily brief; the scope to deal with all the aspects of Islāmic jurisprudence (*fiqh*) and Islāmic law (*sharī'ah*) is limited.

Ibrahim Hewitt, who was the Assistant Director of the *MET* between 1989–1994, prepared and edited some of these fact sheets (apart from the section on surrogacy). The *MET* decided to publish these as a booklet in 1993. The booklet, then titled *What does Islām say about...*, was well received, *alhamdulillāh* (all Praise is for *Allāh*).

In this fourth edition we have made extensive changes and additions to Abortion, Contraception, Divorce, Homosexuality and Sexually Transmittied Deseases like HIV/AIDS. Brother Ibrahim Hewitt has rewritten the topic Muslim Schools and added a new topic entitled Terrorism. We are grateful to M. Alamin for the cover design. I hope this book will continue to benefit those for whom it is intended, especially non-Muslim students and teachers. Any comments and suggestions from readers will help us to improve future editions of the book.

May Almighty *Allāh* reward Ibrahim Hewitt for his contribution. May He also accept the efforts of the *MET* in promoting the understanding of Islām in the West. *Āmīn.*

London
Ṣafar 1425 AH
April 2004 CE

Ghulam Sarwar
Director
The Muslim Educational Trust

Preface

In the Name of Allāh, the Most Merciful, the Most Kind

It is a pleasure to welcome you to the fourth edition of *What does Islām say?* – I hope you find the book informative and useful. Although initially conceived as a series of introductory leaflets prepared in response to students' queries about Islām, the book now reaches a wider audience, *alhamdulillāh*, and readers include students, new Muslims and non-Muslims eager to know more about our way of life.

No book on Islām is entirely comprehensive and so there are areas and topics not covered in these pages. In some cases readers are given a taste of subjects that deserve extensive further study. I do not have the time to do justice to the book by extending it in size, content and accessibility. Keen-eyed readers with copies of previous editions may notice subtle changes in the text as well as shifts in emphasis. Given the nature of life and the human condition this should be expected and I hope that I have been able to incorporate developments in Issues such as Muslim schools and Terrorism to give a broader insight.

Of course, this book is not the result of my efforts alone. I am indebted to my brothers Ghulam Sarwar and Usamah K. ward at the *Muslim Educational Trust*. Both have also enriched the content through their own knowledge. May Allāh reward them both in this life and the next, and may He accept my own small efforts in His way. *Āmīn.*

Leicester   ***Ibrahim Hewitt***
Safar 1425 AH
April 2004 CE

Introduction

Islām is...

- the voluntary submission of one's will to the Will of *Allāh* (God).
- a complete code covering every aspect of life.
- a word derived from the Arabic root-word *silm*, meaning 'submission', 'obedience' and 'peace'.
- the faith of over a fifth of the world's population. Believers in Islām are called Muslims.
- the final revealed religion from *Allāh*.
- based upon five pillars or basic duties:
  1. Affirmation that "there is no god but *Allāh*, Muḥammad is the Messenger of *Allāh*". This is called the *Shahādah*, which in Arabic reads *Lā ilāha ilallāhu, Muḥammadur rasūlullāh*.
  2. Five compulsory daily prayers, called *Ṣalāh*.
  3. Fasting during the daylight hours (dawn to sunset) of the month of *Ramaḍān*. This is called *Ṣawm*.
  4. Payment of 2½ percent per annum of one's annual savings to the poor. This is called *Zakāh*.
  5. Pilgrimage to *Makkah* at the appointed time, if it can be afforded and one is physically capable, at least once in a lifetime. This is the *Ḥajj*.

Muslims believe...

- that there is only one God – *Allāh* – the Creator of the universe.
- that Muḥammad ﷺ is the final messenger and prophet of *Allāh* sent to mankind.
- that *Allāh* has sent many prophets to mankind before Muḥammad ﷺ, including Nuḥ (Noah), Ibrāhīm (Abraham), Mūsā (Moses), Dāwūd (David) and 'Īsā (Jesus), peace be upon them, all calling with a universal message to the worship of Allāh.
- in the *Qur'ān* as the final, perfectly preserved revelation of *Allāh's* guidance for mankind, sent through the Angel Jibrā'īl (Gabriel) to Muḥammad ﷺ.
- that books of guidance were revealed to Prophets Mūsā, Dāwūd and 'Īsā, namely: the *Tawrāt*, the *Zabūr* and the *Injīl*; but the original message they contained was distorted by men. Hence, whilst Muslims must believe in the original revelation and existence of these books, they do not believe that the 'equivalent' books in the Bible – the Torah, Psalms and Gospels – have preserved the original revelation.
- in the Angels of *Allāh*, who always carry out *Allāh's* commands and cannot disobey Him.
- in the Day of Judgement when everyone will be resurrected and brought to account for their own actions in this worldly life.
- in Life after Death (*Ākhirah*); in Paradise (*Jannah*), and Hell (*Jahannam*); in *Allāh's* justice and His reward and punishment.

Abortion

While Islām for certain valid reasons does allow for the prevention of pregnancy through means such as contraception, Muslim jurists unanimously agree that once a foetus is completely formed and deemed alive, aborting it is strongly prohibited (Ḥarām). This is because abortion in such cases constitutes an offence against a living human being and human life in Islam is sacrosanct.

Do not take life –
which Allāh has made sacred –
except for just cause.
{Al-Qur'ān, chapter 17, verse 33}

On that account We ordained for the Children of Israel
that if any one slew a person –
unless it be for murder or for spreading mischief in the land –
it would be as if he slew the whole people.
And if any one saved a life
it would be as if he saved the life of the whole people.
{Al-Qur'ān, chapter 5, verse 32}

We have honoured the sons of Ādam... {Al-Qur'ān, chapter 17, verse 70}

There is scholarly debate amongst Muslims about the exact point a human foetus could be deemed to have life; this is because of differences of interpretation of a prophetic saying regarding the time at which the soul enters the human body (See: Al-Bukhārī Vol. 9 p.411. See also Zarabozo's commentary on Forty Ḥadīth, Ḥadīth No. 4, Vol. 1, p.387 onwards, and. p.408 onwards). Some scholars state the process to begin 40 days after conception while others say it is 120. In either case, abortion is prohibited except under exceptional circumstances, which may include: rape, foetal deformity of the type of anencephaly (no brain), congenital rubella, specific mental, physical complications for the mother.

The Human Fertilisation and Embryology Act 1990 allows abortion on the following conditions (See section 37: Amendment of law relating to termination of pregnancy):

1) That the pregnancy has not exceeded its twenty-fourth week and that the continuance of the pregnancy would involve risk, greater than if the pregnancy were terminated, of injury to the physical or mental health of the pregnant woman or any existing children of the family; or

2) That the termination is necessary to prevent grave permanent injury to the physical or mental health of the pregnant woman; or

3) That the continuance of the pregnancy would involve risk to the life of the pregnant woman greater than if the pregnancy were terminated; or

4) That there is a substantial risk that if the child were born it would suffer from such physical or mental abnormalities as to be seriously handicapped.

It should also be noted that although UK law (The Human Fertilisation and Embryology Act 1990) allows abortion as long as the foetus has not exceeded its twenty-fourth week, premature babies at 20 -23 weeks have demonstrated survival within hospitals in this country. The Law is not applied as it should be. It is widely accepted that in practice, women in the UK get abortion on demand.

In the modern world where ultrasound scanners can detect from the sixth week whether the foetus is male or female, babies are becoming increasingly vulnerable in certain parts of the world where abortions may be carried out simply because the child is female. In some regions such infanticide is seriously affecting the balance of the population.

In Arabia before the advent of Islām the tribal custom was to bury unwanted baby girls alive. This abominable practice was totally prohibited and there are two verses of the Qur'ān connected with that which could also be applied directly to the circumstances of abortion:

> **Slay not your children, fearing a fall to poverty,**
> **We shall provide for them and for you.**
> **Lo! the slaying of them is a great sin** {Al-Qur'ān, chapter 17, verse 31}
> **When the female (infant), buried alive, is questioned –**
> **For what crime was she killed?** {Al-Qur'ān, chapter 81, verses 8–9}

Those who advocate the belief that abortion is permissible because 'a woman has the right to decide what she does with her own body' should remember that it is not just 'her own body' but also the body of another; as the mother of an unborn child, there is a separate but totally dependent living human being inside her created by the Will of *Allāh*, entitled to her utmost care and protection. If, for any reason, the mother fears the pregnancy is too much to bear, then it is up to the family, the community and society at large to give her every support and comfort. But that child's life must not be deliberately ended.

If, however, it is reliably established that the continuation of the pregnancy will result in the death of the mother, then the principle of choosing the lesser of two evils is followed, and an abortion is allowable. The mother's life takes precedence over that of her baby in such an instance because the mother is already established in life with many duties and responsibilities. It is thus less disruptive to family life (although just as regrettable) to sacrifice the life of the unborn child which has not yet acquired a personality nor has any duties, responsibilities or obligations. Abortion is also linked to the increased risk of breast cancer.

The widespread availability of abortion has meant the slaughter of millions of unborn children. Recent statistics released by the Goverment pertaining to legal abortions carried out under the 1967 Abortion Act in 2002 show over 175,500 abortions taking place within England and Wales with over 3,500 of them consisting of girls aged 15 and under (See: Office of National Statistics, Abortion Statistics, England and Wales: 2002, Tables 1 and 2). This staggering figure does not include abortions carried out by non-residents and the large number of underground abortions carried out on the basis of perceived 'physical deformities'. The murder of these tiny human beings could have been avoided by behaving correctly and obeying *Allāh's* laws.

Adoption

In Islām, the issue of adoption must be looked at in the light of the structure of the family, the inheritance laws and the laws concerning relationships and marriage. Islām is very clear about these matters and so great care has to be taken when considering situations such as adoption.

Of course, taking an orphan or a homeless child into your own home to care for and educate is an act of great merit.

> **Prophet Muḥammad ﷺ said, "I and the one who raises an orphan will be like these two [pointing to his index and middle fingers] in Paradise."** {Al-Bukhāri, Muslim}

In other words, such a person will be very close to the Prophet ﷺ in the Hereafter, something all Muslims pray for.

In pre-Islāmic Arabia (and in other parts of the world), it was common practice for people to call anyone their 'son' and that person automatically took on the rights of a real son. This was condemned by *Allāh* in the *Qur'ān* because of the possible confusion and wrongs which could arise from such an unreal relationship. This is where the considerations mentioned above must be looked at.

For example, once this 'adopted son' has reached the age of puberty he would, under Islāmic law, be forbidden to mix socially with the women in the household with whom he has no blood link and he is not their relative, so they must wear full Islāmic dress in front of him, something they would not do in front of their own sons, brothers, nephews, uncles and others to whom they are prohibited from being married. The same would be true for a girl who would have to wear Islāmic dress at all times in front of her 'adopted father' and the male members of the family to whom she could be married because of the missing close blood link. An exception to this would be if the adopted child is taken into the family home as a baby and is suckled by the mother of the house. After reaching adulthood the adopted child would then be unable to marry any of its 'brothers' or 'sisters' who had suckled from the same mother and would thus be able to mix in the home as a close member of the family.

The laws of inheritance in Islām are also very clear, and every relative has a right to receive a set portion of the estate. An 'adopted child' cannot, as of right, make a claim on the deceased 'parent's' estate unless the person has made provision for such a settlement out of the part of the estate left for bequests, etc. in their will.

It is wrong to adopt someone and give them your family name as if they are blood members of the family, saying "this is my son" or "this is my daughter", especially if their birth parents are known. Islām is very similar to present-day thinking concerning adoption in this respect; it is important for adopted children to know they are adopted and, if possible, who their birth parents are. If such facts are kept away from them it is perfectly possible for heartbreak and confusion to arise as young adults.

For example, imagine that a brother and sister have been separated for adoption as very young children and both grow-up in ignorance of the circumstances of their adoption. Imagine that they meet in later life and are sexually attracted to the point of contemplating marriage. Such a scenario is not beyond the bounds of possibility and will be avoided if the Islāmic way is followed. "He is not my son but I will look after him as if he was" should be the correct way to move forward in adoption cases.

It could be said that, in Islām, long-term fostering rather than outright adoption may be the more suitable option, although this carries a risk of instability for the child and the family. It should not be outside the realms of possibility, though, for legal safeguards to be built in to any long-term fostering arrangement to ensure that all concerned share a sense of 'permanence' and stability.

Animal Welfare

Islām lays great emphasis on animal welfare and the responsibility human beings have to look after other creatures. There are many verses in the *Qur'ān* and the sayings of Prophet Muḥammad ﷺ concerning this issue.

There is not an animal (that lives) on the Earth,
nor a being that flies on its wings,
but (forms part of) communities like you.
Nothing have We omitted from the Book,
and they (all) shall be gathered to their Lord in the end.
{Al-Qur'ān, chapter 6, verse 38}

The Prophet ﷺ said, "One who kills even a sparrow or anything smaller without a justifiable reason will be answerable to Allāh." When asked what would be a justifiable reason he replied, "To slaughter it for food – not to kill and discard it." {Aḥmad, An-Nasā'ī}

Human beings, even when they do not obey the commands of *Allāh*, still benefit from *Allāh's* consideration for the welfare of animals, as is shown in this warning from Prophet Muhammad ﷺ:

"If people should withhold Zakāh, you should realise that this has never happened without the rain being stopped from falling, and were it not for the animals' sake it would never rain again." {Ibn Mājah}

Showing kindness to animals is an act of great virtue, and can lead to the forgiveness of sins by *Allāh*:

Prophet Muhammad ﷺ said, "A prostitute was forgiven by Allāh, because, passing by a panting dog near a well and seeing that the dog was about to die of thirst, she took off her shoe, and tying it with her head-cover she drew out some water for it. So, Allāh forgave her because of that." {Al-Bukhārī}

On the other hand, cruelty to animals is a sin, which may lead to punishment in the Hereafter:

Prophet Muhammad ﷺ said, "A woman was punished and put into Hell because of a cat which she had kept locked till it died of hunger. Allāh said (to the woman), 'You neither fed her nor watered her when you locked it up, nor did you set her free to eat the insects of the earth.'"
{Al-Bukhārī, Muslim}

Branding or beating animals provoked the following response from Prophet Muhammad ﷺ:

"May Allāh condemn the one who branded it (a donkey, on its face)." {Muslim}

One day, the Prophet ﷺ passed by a camel that was so thin that its back had shrunk to its belly. He said,

"Fear Allāh in these beasts – ride them in good health and free them from work while they are still in good health." {Abū Dāwūd}

The Prophet ﷺ said,

"It is a great sin for man to imprison those animals which are in his power." {Muslim}

A further narration shows how we must be considerate to animals:

We were with the Messenger of Allāh ﷺ during a journey. We saw a bird with her two young ones and we captured her young ones. The bird came and began to spread its wings. The Messenger of Allāh ﷺ came and said, "Who grieved this for its young ones? Return its young ones to it." He also saw an ant village that we had burnt. He asked, "Who has burnt this?" We replied, "We did." He said, "It is not proper to punish with fire except the Lord of fire." {Abū Dāwūd}

It is reported that the Prophet ﷺ condemned those who mutilate any part of any animal whilst it is still alive. {Aḥmad}

The Prophet ﷺ also forbade the setting up of animals to fight each other {Abū Dāwūd, At-Tirmidhī} and condemned those who pinion or restrain animals in any other way for the purpose of target shooting. {Muslim}

Calendar

**It is He [Allāh] Who made the Sun to be a shining glory
and the Moon to be a light (of beauty),
and measured out stages for her;
that ye might know the number of years
and the count (of time).**
{Al-Qur'ān, chapter 10, verse 5}

The Sun and the Moon follow courses (exactly) computed.
{Al-Qur'ān, chapter 55, verse 5}

The Islāmic calendar is a lunar calendar, that is, based on the cycle of the Moon. An Islāmic year has twelve months, each of either 29 or 30 days, so the number of days in the year is about 354, 11 days shorter than the Western solar year. This is why Islāmic events and festivals cycle through the seasons, and appear to be earlier each year compared to the Western calendar. Islāmic years date from the *hijrah* (migration) of the Prophet ﷺ in 622 CE.

The months of the Islāmic year are:

Muḥarram
Ṣafar
Rabī'ul-Awwal
Rabī'ul-Ākhir
Jumādal-Ūlā
Jumādal-Ākhirah
Rajab
Sha'bān
Ramaḍān
Shawwāl
Dhul-Qa'dah
Dhul-Ḥijjah

The months *Muḥarram*, *Rajab*, *Dhū al-Qa'dah* and *Dhū al-Ḥijjah* are sacred months.

The Prophet ﷺ said, "Time has taken its original shape which it had when Allāh created the Heaven and the Earth. The year is of twelve months, four of which are sacred, and out of these (four) three are in succession, i.e. Dhū al-Qa'dah, Dhū al-Ḥijjah and Muḥarram, and the fourth is Rajab which is named after the Muḍar tribe, between (the month of) Jumāda' (al-Ākhirah) and Sha'bān." {Al-Bukhāri, Abū Dāwūd}

The start and end of each month depend on the sighting of the new moon. If, after 29 days, the new moon is sighted then the next month begins. If the new moon is not sighted, the current month continues for one further day before the next month begins. So a month will have either 29 or 30 days. When calculating festival dates, then, it is important to allow a day or two either way to allow for variations in the sighting of the new moon. Authorities responsible for setting the dates of examinations and other important events should particularly note this variation in the Muslim calendar. [*see also* CRESCENT]

Capital Punishment

**... take not life, which *Allāh* has made sacred,
except by way of justice and law...** {Al-Qur'ān, chapter 6, verse 151}

The laws on crime and punishment are, like many other things relating to Islām, often misinterpreted by non-Muslims as being unduly harsh, cruel and 'barbaric'. However, Islāmic law in this respect is there to ensure that not only is justice done, but it is also seen to be done. The welfare of the whole society must be looked after, and those who would disturb social order must be deterred.

Any crime that destabilises society is viewed seriously and has serious consequences for the guilty person. Three crimes carry the death penalty in an Islāmic society: murder, adultery by a married person and apostasy. Prophet Muḥammad ﷺ said:

"The shedding of the blood of a Muslim is not lawful except for one of three reasons: a life for a life, a married person who commits zinā [adultery] and one who turns aside from his religion and abandons the community." {Al-Bukhārī, Muslim}

A murderer is an obvious threat to society and that threat must be removed. The family of the deceased may pardon the murderer, who would then be spared the death penalty, and may then be required to go to prison, and perhaps pay compensation to the next-of-kin. Giving the relatives of the victim a say in the punishment of the murderer is an important part of the Islāmic legal system.

An Islāmic society is based upon strong family ties between husband, wife and children. Adultery shatters such ties with catastrophic consequences for the family and society at large (divorces, family break-ups, one-parent families in need of state support, etc.). Hence, adultery also carries a very serious penalty.

For the crime of apostasy, it should be borne in mind that in an Islāmic State, Islām *is the basis of* the State, not just the State religion. Any act of apostasy that results in open rebellion against Islām is, therefore, an act of treason. Even in Britain, the penalty for high treason is death.

Obviously, it is vital that the question of guilt is not in doubt before a sentence is carried out, and only the proper authorities in the country can implement the due process of law prescribed by the *Sharī'ah* (Islāmic law).

With accusations of adultery, at least four witnesses are required to the actual act of adultery, something which will rarely be possible (at least in a civilised society) since the adultery must virtually take place in a public place if the required witnesses are to be available. If the required witnesses are not available, then the person making the accusation of adultery must be punished for slandering the moral standards of fellow Muslims. Freely-given confessions of guilt, repeated four times in court are acceptable proof in place of the witnesses.

Contraception

Contraception is seen by some as being the best way to allow young people to experiment with sexuality without the fear of unwanted pregnancy. Although contraception is often called 'planned parenthood', the way this has been imposed at the behest of the International Monetary Fund (IMF), the World Bank and the United Nations Educational, Scientific and Cultural Organisation (UNESCO) may be called 'forced population control' mainly for economic and political reasons. Such policy is in conflict with a basic Islamic human right and it is the consensus of Muslim scholars that no population control policy should be applied on people.

In a society where extramarital and premarital sex are forbidden and there is no free-mixing between adult men and women, contraception as the means to prevent pregnancy becomes less necessary. However, the fact that contraception unlike abortion does not involve the killing of an already existing foetus has led to a great majority of Muslim jurists having tolerant views towards it.

Imām Ghazālī (1058–1111) drew a clear distinction between contraception and abortion: "Contraception is not like abortion. Abortion is a crime against an existing being. Existence has various stages. The first is the settling of the semen in the womb and its mixing with the secretions [egg] of the woman. It is then ready to receive life. Disturbing it is a crime. When it develops further and becomes a lump, abortion is a greater crime. When it acquires a soul and its creation is complete the crime becomes even more grievous. The crime reaches its maximum seriousness after the foetus is separated from its mother alive." (Al-Ihyā', book of An-Nikāḥ [Marriage], p.74). Ghazālī wrote about the permissibility of contraception and enumerated a wide range of conditions under which it could be practised, these generally included health hazards and specific socio-economic factors although such contraception is highly discouraged.

As for those who fear they would not be able to provide for the child should they become pregnant, they may take heart by considering Allāh's promise in the Qur'an:

... No soul shall have a burden laid on it greater than it can bear.
No mother shall be treated unfairly on account of her child.
Nor father on account of his child. {Al-Qur'ān, chapter 2, verse 233}

In specific cases where contraception is allowed in Islam, mutual consent is a condition.

"A man must not practise withdrawal ('Azl) with his wife unless she freely consents." {Ibn Mājah, Ḥadīth 1918 www.al-islam.com (Arabic)}

It is interesting to note that outcries about shortage of resources in the face of population growth conveniently sidetrack complementary solutions such as the redistribution of wealth on both a national and international level, the reduction in military expenditure and an allocation of more resources towards humanitarian causes.

It should be borne in mind that contraception is not always reliable or safe, either in preventing pregnancy or the transmission of diseases (STDs). Condoms, which could be loosely equated with *coitus interruptus ('Azl)*, do not give 100% protection. Some Muslim jurists allow *coitus interruptus* on the basis of some of the sayings of Prophet Muḥammad ﷺ. The 'Pill' has recently been linked to harmful side effects, such as an increased risk of breast cancer. It is the intention which is important in making a decision about contraception. Practising Muslims will always put their total trust in Allāh and live a decent life, trying their best to emulate the *Sunnah* of the Prophet ﷺ. We must remember that no human being has the power to stop what *Allāh* wills to happen. Regarding the practice of coitus interruptus, the Prophet ﷺ remarked:

"If you wish so you may. And if Allah willed for her something (pregnancy), she will have it." {Muslim Vol. 2, Ḥadīth 3383, p. 734}

Crescent

He [*Allāh*] has made subject to you
the Night and the Day,
the Sun and the Moon;
and the stars are in subjection by His Command:
verily in this are Signs for men who are wise.
{Al-Qur'ān, chapter 16, verse 12}

Among His Signs are the Night and the Day,
and the Sun and the Moon.
Adore not the Sun and the Moon,
but adore *Allāh*, Who created them,
if it is Him you wish to serve. {Al-Qur'ān, chapter 41, verse 37}

The Moon is one of the many parts of nature referred to in the *Qur'ān*. Yet the crescent of the new moon has become associated particularly as a symbol of Islam. Its status is not similar to the Christian cross: the crescent moon is not uniquely significant in

Islam, nor do Muslims hold a great attachment to it. If nothing else, it has become a convenient symbol.

The crescent has appeared in Islamic architectural designs from the early days of Islam, notably as one of many features in the Dome of the Rock (*Qubbat As-Sakhrah*) in Jerusalem (*Al-Quds*). It was used as a symbol of the Byzantine empire, and on the standards and flags of the Ottoman Turks. It became a symbol of the Ottoman empire, and eventually was used in the Muslim world in general. A number of national flags of Muslim countries incorporate the crescent, and it is used by the *Red Crescent* organisation, the banner under which the *Red Cross* operates in Muslim countries.

The greatest significance of the Moon to Muslims is in the calculation of the Islamic calendar, which is a lunar calendar, each month beginning after the sighting of the crescent of the new moon. [*see also CALENDAR*]

Divorce

Unlike many marriages in the West, where premarital love and intimacy are increasingly common, the basic ingredient for a successful Muslim marriage is a shared set of values upon which to build a life together. A shared belief in *Islam* can often bind couples together in their relationship allowing them to withstand many of the pressures exerted by contemporary Western societies which eventually force many couples apart. Prophet Muhammad ﷺ said:

> *"Of all things which have been permitted, divorce is the most hated by Allah."* {Abū Dāwūd, Hadith. 2173. The Hadith Software Version 1.0 }

A Muslim marriage is seen as a real relationship between two individuals who cannot, realistically, be expected to be 100% immune from the stress and strain of everyday life. Islam's emphasis is on the continuation of a marriage which ensures happiness, love, warmth and contentment, and the welfare of children. Their shared faith will help to cushion a Muslim couple from the worst effects of marital problems. Nevertheless, Islam is realistic enough to prepare couples for the possibility that they might not be able to carry on together as husband and wife, for a variety of reasons, and so divorce – although disliked – is allowed when all conciliatory efforts have failed. It is essential that a marriage should be harmonious and not injurious to the life and health of the couple and their families and, ultimately, society at large.

In 2002, the number of divorces granted in the UK increased by 1.9 per cent, from 157,000 in 2001 to 160,000. There is an increasing trend within the UK and across most of Europe of falling marriage rates and marital breakdown. (See: Office for National

Statistics, UK, www.statistics.gov.uk). Such an increase could be due to an increasingly relaxed attitude towards marriage and what sort of commitment it entails. This results in divorces on the slightest grounds, namely 'behavioural issues'. This type of attitude is against Islāmic teachings which encourage patience to sustain a marriage.

The other extreme can be seen in some cultures where divorce is totally prohibited, often resulting in drastic consequence: "Indian Government statistics show that husbands and in-laws killed nearly 7,000 women in 2001 over inadequate dowry payments." (See: 'India's dowry deaths', http://news.bbc.co.uk/1/hi/programmes/crossing_continents/3071963.stm , as updated till 16 July 2003) . In many cases such deaths could have been avoided except for the stigma attached to divorce compelling the bride to live intolerable conditions eventually resulting in her death.

Islam shows the middle path: it permits divorce, as sometimes it is the only solution to serious problems of marital discord, yet it discourages a flippant relaxed attitude that advcoates divorce on any pretext whatsoever. A husband who dislikes a certain trait in his wife might discover that she possesses other qualities that appeal to him.

The Qur'ān provides general guidelines for the process of divorce upholding the values of justice, fairness and kindness. (Al-Qur'ān, chapter 2: 227–237, chapter 65:1–12)

The regulations of Islam on family life, matrimony, and the respective positions of men and women, serve as a model which all nations would do well to emulate.

Drugs and Alcohol

Prophet Muḥammad ﷺ said,
"Every intoxicant is khamr
and every khamr is ḥarām [forbidden]." {Muslim}

Any substance that clouds the mind or impairs reasoning, perception or discernment is forbidden in Islām (unless used for a vital medical requirement, such as a general anaesthetic). Indeed, anyone involved in any part of the production or selling of drugs or alcohol, whether they use the stuff themselves or not, has been cursed by Prophet Muḥammad ﷺ.

The *Qur'ān* was revealed in stages over a period of 23 years with various pieces of legislation for the Muslim community arriving at the time when their faith was strong enough to accept them. For example, at first it was said that the bad in *khamr* outweighed any beneficial aspects; then Muslims were told not to pray whilst affected by *khamr*, i.e. drunk or otherwise intoxicated; then, finally, the following verses were revealed:

O you who believe!
Truly, intoxicants and gambling,
[dedication of] stones and [divination by] arrows
are an abomination of Satan's handiwork:
avoid such abomination in order that you may prosper.
Satan's plan is to sow enmity and hatred among you
with intoxicants and gambling,
and to hinder you from the remembrance of *Allāh*
and from *Ṣalāh* [obligatory prayer].
Will you not then abstain?
{Al-Qur'ān, chapter 5, verses 90-91}

Alcohol and other drugs, such as cannabis, Ecstasy, cocaine, heroin, etc. are definitely included in the category of *khamr*. Apart from the fact that such substances are generally taken as a means of escape from the realities of life into the realms of fantasy, which alone confirms what *Allāh* says in the above verses (*...and to hinder you from the remembrance of Allāh...*), there are serious physical, psychological and moral effects arising from the use of drugs. In today's society, such effects are well documented: violence, crime, premature death and family break-ups to name but a few.

Prophet Muḥammad ﷺ said, "Do not drink wine – it is the key to every evil." {Al-Bukhārī}

Indeed, alcoholic drinks, which in Britain and many other countries are socially accepted stimulants, have a profoundly detrimental impact on society. In Britain alcohol is a factor in: 70% of homicides, 43% of assaults and 82% of incidences of disorder (*The Times*, 4 April 1996); 30% of road accidents (*The Guardian*, 16 January 1996) and 14% of road deaths (*The Independent*, 5 December 1996) - that's 10 road deaths every week; one third of 16–19 year old pedestrians killed on the roads (*The Guardian*, 16 January 1996); 33% of child abuse cases and 40% of domestic violence incidents (*The Times Educational Supplement*, 14 November 1997); and 61% of all suicides (*The Independent*, 19 September 1995). About 2.8 million people in Britain are alcohol dependent, and alcohol misuse costs British industry £2 billion per year and the health service £150 million per year; 28,000 deaths per year are alcohol related – well over 500 every week – as are a quarter of all hospital admissions (*The Independent*, 19 September 1995). It has been calculated that alcohol causes 10 times more damage to young people than drugs (*The Times*, 22 November 1996). This is just part of the price paid for mere enjoyment – alcoholic drinks are not a necessity. Just as *Allāh* says in the *Qur'ān*, the harm outweighs the benefit. The manufacturers of alcoholic drinks, not content with their already vast profits, are cynically targeting young people with 'alcopops' – sweet, strong drinks that are very trendy and appealing, especially to 'underage' drinkers (below the age of 18).

Drugs such as heroin, apart from wrecking the lives of users, their families and their communities, cause addicts to turn to crime so they can support their habits. Drug addicts are responsible for £4 billion of crime each year in Britain, despite the annual £1.4 billion spent on prevention and rehabilitation (*The Times*, 28 April 1998). Whilst boys steal so that they can buy the drugs they need, many girls addicted to drugs turn to prostitution.

Hence, anyone who uses *khamr* has the potential to become a diseased member of society totally incapable of fulfilling any of the obligations and responsibilities everyone has towards their fellow human beings.

It is the general rule in Islām that it is forbidden for a Muslim to do anything that may cause his or her own death, or inflict any personal damage on oneself. [*see also* SUICIDE] The life, health and wealth of a person do not belong to them; they are entrusted with such bounties by *Allāh*, the Creator. Hence, every human being has a duty to look after what *Allāh* has given them. *Allāh* makes this very clear in the *Qur'ān*:

...nor kill (or destroy) yourselves;
for verily, *Allāh* has been merciful to you.
{Al-Qur'ān, chapter 4, verse 29}

And make not your own hands
contribute to your destruction... *{Al-Qur'ān, chapter 2, verse 195}*

In addition, Prophet Muḥammad ﷺ said:

"Do not harm yourself or others." *{Aḥmad, Ibn Mājah}*

On the basis of the above, some Muslim scholars have declared that the use of tobacco is *ḥarām* (forbidden), although others say smoking tobacco is 'only' *makrūh* – not *ḥarām* but extremely disliked – because they are not convinced of the dangers of smoking cigarettes and other tobacco-related substances. However, the overwhelming weight of evidence proves that smoking is bad for the health of the smoker, the children of smokers, and those who inadvertently breathe in the smoke (passive smoking). In September 2003, the BBC reported that almost 5 million people a year die from smoking-related diseases around the world; that is almost 14,000 per day, a shocking statistic in any language.

Environmental Issues

And the Firmament has He [*Allāh*] raised high,
and He has set up the Balance,
in order that you may not transgress (due) balance. {*Al-Qur'ān,*
chapter 55, verses 7-8}

The planet that we live on has been created by *Allāh* and entrusted to mankind until the Day of Judgement. As His 'agents' (*Khalā'ifah*) on Earth, we have the responsibility of looking after all the other creatures, the plants, the atmosphere and everything else that surrounds us. It is important, therefore, for Muslims to play a leading part in the efforts to protect our environment. Life on Earth is set up with natural balance and this is the key to our survival here.

Allāh has created other planets which are unable to sustain life because that balance is missing. Anything we do which upsets or damages the balance of the life cycle here on Earth will have to be answered for in the Hereafter.

Allāh says in the *Qur'ān*:

It is He [*Allāh*] who has made you Agents [*Khalā'ifah*],
Inheritors of the Earth. {*Al-Qur'ān, chapter 6, verse 165*}

It is *Allāh* who has subjected the sea to you...
and He has subjected to you, as from Him,
all that is in the Heavens and the Earth... {*Al-Qur'ān, chapter 45,*
verses 12-13}

Prophet Muḥammad ﷺ said: "The world is sweet and green
(alluring) and verily Allāh is going to install you as vicegerent
in it in order to see how you act." {*Muslim*}

We can see the effects of mankind's inability to look after what *Allāh* has bestowed upon us all over the world: pollution, extinction, deforestation, etc. In the rush to make money we are turning once fertile lands into deserts, and rainforests into pastures. The short-term 'benefits' in terms of cash crops or cattle feed will be far outweighed by the long-term damage to the Earth's atmosphere and eco-structure. The balance mentioned in the *Qur'ān* is tilting too far away from normality. Life is becoming increasingly unsustainable and abnormal.

Muslims must make every effort to be 'green' and to help to slow down and halt the present destructive trends in society. Political and material decisions must not be taken without due consideration for the side-effects of what is planned, and the guiding hand behind all decisions should be the guidance given to mankind by *Allāh* in the *Qur'ān* and the example of Prophet Muḥammad ﷺ.

Festivals

There are two authentic Islāmic festivals annually: *ʿĪd ul Fiṭr* and *ʿĪd ul Aḍḥā*.

ʿĪdul Fiṭr

This is a celebration of the completion of the month of fasting in *Ramaḍān*, and is on the first day of the next month, *Shawwāl*. It is an occasion of great joy, mixed with a tinge of sadness at the passing of the blessed month of *Ramaḍān*.

The day begins with a light meal, after which the family will go to a special *ʿĪd* prayer. If the weather is not too cold or wet, this prayer may be held outdoors, in a field or park. Otherwise, it will be in the mosque. After the prayer, the *Imām* (who leads the prayer) gives a short talk.

People wear their best clothes for *ʿĪd*. Young people particularly delight in buying new clothes especially for *ʿĪd* day, if their families can afford it.

After prayer the rest of the day is spent visiting friends and relatives. Everyone will try to serve special food and as Muslims come from every race and nationality, the foods served on that day will reflect the particular cultural background of the family. As such, there is no specific Islāmic or *ʿĪd* food or dish.

Ramaḍān is a month when the giving of charity is particularly encouraged. In the last few days of *Ramaḍān* all Muslims, young or old, give enough food for a meal (or its equivalent), which is then distributed amongst the poor and needy on *ʿĪdul Fiṭr*. This is known as *Zakāt ul Fiṭr*, and it enables the poor and the needy to share in the joy of *ʿĪd*.

ʿĪdul Aḍḥā

This is on the 10th day of the month of *Dhul-Ḥijjah*, and is followed by three further days of celebration called *Tashrīq*. It is at this time that the pilgrimage to *Makkah* culminates for the millions completing the annual *Ḥajj*.

This celebration commemorates the willingness of Prophet Ibrāhīm (Abraham) to sacrifice his oldest son, Ismāʿīl (Ishmael) – not his second son Isḥāq (Isaac), as is wrongly claimed in the Bible. *Allāh* was pleased that Ibrāhīm and Ismāʿīl were willing to obey His command, and so ordered that a lamb should be sacrificed instead of Ismāʿīl.

Just as on *ʿĪdul Fiṭr*, there is a special *ʿĪd* prayer in the morning. After the prayer every family arranges to have an animal slaughtered, such as a sheep, goat, cow or camel. The meat of the sacrificed animal is shared amongst relatives, neighbours and the poor.

People again wear their best clothes. During these days people try to visit as many of their relatives, neighbours and friends as possible.

Other occasions

During the last ten days of *Ramaḍān* there is a special night called *Lailatul Qadr* (The Night of Decrees or Power). The *Qur'ān* describes this night as being better than a thousand months. It is a night which many Muslims try to spend in prayer, seeking the pleasure of *Allāh*. Its exact night is not known, other than it is on an odd-numbered night within the last ten days of *Ramaḍān*.

Although there are other occasions in the calendar of historical or cultural significance to Muslims, they do not form a part of Islām as such, though some Muslims may hold celebrations or special events.

Food and Drink

Food and drink have direct effects on our health so Islām, which aims at the establishment of a healthy society, lays down guidelines and regulations about what is good for us to eat. Our physical health matters as well as our moral health. *Allāh* makes it clear in the *Qur'ān*:

> O Mankind, eat of the lawful and good things
> from what is in the Earth
> and do not follow the footsteps of the devil.
> Surely, he is your open enemy. {Al-Qur'ān, chapter 2, verse 168}

The Arabic word for 'lawful' is *ḥalāl*; 'unlawful' is *ḥarām*. In another part of the *Qur'ān*, *Allāh* makes it quite clear what is *ḥalāl* and *ḥarām* for us to eat:

> O you who believe!
> Eat of the good things that We have provided for you,
> and be thankful to *Allāh*
> if it is He alone whom you worship.
> Indeed, what He has forbidden to you
> is the flesh of dead animals
> and blood and the flesh of swine,
> and that which has been sacrificed
> to anyone other than *Allāh*.
> But if one is compelled by necessity,
> neither craving [it] nor transgressing,

there is no sin on him;
indeed, *Allāb* is Forgiving, Merciful. *{Al-Qur'ān, chapter 2, verse 172-173}*

From these verses we can see that, basically, four things have been deemed *ḥarām*: the flesh of carrion; blood; pig meat (pork); and meat from any animal not slaughtered in the name of *Allāb*. By implication, any produce derived from the above or any food containing or cooked in or with such things will also be *ḥarām*.

All seafood is *ḥalāl*. *Allāb* says in the *Qur'ān*:

**Lawful to you is the pursuit of water-game
and its use for food...** *{Al-Qur'ān, chapter 5, verse 96}*

This verse is further clarified by the following *ḥadīth* (saying) of Prophet Muḥammad ﷺ: Jābir reported that the Prophet ﷺ once sent some of his companions on an expedition. They found a dead whale by the sea and subsisted on it for more than twenty days. When they returned to *Madīnah* they told the Prophet ﷺ about this and he said:

"Eat the food which Allāb has brought forth for you and feed us from it if you have any left." *{Al-Bukhārī}*

He ﷺ also said of the sea:

"Its water is pure and what dies in it is lawful food."
{Abū Dāwūd, At-Tirmidhī, Ibn Mājah, An-Nasā'ī}

Islāmic law requires an animal to be slain by the use of a sharp knife penetrating the inner part of the animal's neck to allow the maximum drainage of blood. The name of *Allāb* must be invoked at the time of cutting and the act must be done out of sight of any other animals awaiting slaughter. The method of slaughter is similar to that used by the Jews (producing kosher meat) and so if no *'ḥalāl'* meat is available, kosher meat is acceptable for Muslims. Animals must not be fed impure or inappropriate substances. In Britain, cows that had been fed the remains of diseased sheep developed a virulent fatal disease (BSE – *Bovine Spongiform Encephalopathy*), which appears to have been transmitted to human beings (CJD – *Creutz'feldt Jacob Disease*).

Intoxicants of any kind are also *ḥarām*, even in small quantities. Prophet Muḥammad ﷺ said:

"Of that which intoxicates in a large amount, a small amount is ḥarām." *{Aḥmad, Abū Dāwūd, At-Tirmidhī}*

Alcohol should not form part of the ingredients of any food prepared for Muslims. [*see also* DRUGS AND ALCOHOL]

All vegetables are *halāl* and therefore vegetarian food is acceptable to Muslims (but remember the alcohol prohibition mentioned above).

Muslims come from every corner of the globe and the style of dishes prepared by Muslims varies enormously. It should not be taken for granted that *halāl* food = curry, or curry = *halāl* (you could, for example, have curried pork, clearly not *halāl*). Even traditional English food can be *halāl*: fish and chips, for example, is perfectly *halāl* provided the ingredients are not cooked in the same oil used for *harām* items such as pork sausages, something which tends to happen in many fish and chip shops in Britain.

Homosexuality

Section 28 of the Local Government Act 1988 prohibited local authorities from intentionally promoting homosexuality or publishing material with that intention and from promoting the teaching in any maintained school of the acceptability of homosexuality. This section was repealed in 2003, because of the pressure created by homosexual lobbies, with slogans such as "coming out of the closet" and "sexual liberty and freedom". Pressure formed by these lobbies on political and legal institutions, the media, and society in general has resulted in a radically different definition and concept of homosexuality in the mindset of the common person in Britain. **Legislation proposals contained in the Queen's speech given on 27 November 2003, allowing for the registration of civil partnerships between same-sex couples, went almost unnoticed amidst a furore about escalating university tuition fees**. Equally shocking was the recent consecration of the first openly gay bishop within the Anglican church in the United States (See: Profile of Gene Robinson, The Guardian, October 31 2003). Such legislative proposals sound the death knell for marriage and family life, having catastrophic social, economical and moral consequences.

Up until 1970 the British psychiatric establishment broadly classified homosexuality as a 'mental disorder'. In 1973 the Nomenclature Committee of the *Diagnostic and Statistical Manual of Mental Disorders (DSM)*, the official reference book for diagnosing mental disorders in America and throughout much of the world, responding to pressure from homosexual activist groups, voted for the elimination of 'homosexuality' from its official diagnostic categories of mental illness. (See: "An Instant Cure", *Time* magazine, 1 April 1974, p. 45)

Islām, like most other major faiths of the world, categorically forbids homosexual practices (sexual relations between two men or between two women), regarding them as a great sin. In a society under Islāmic law, such would be severely punished.

Of all the creatures in the world,
will you approach males,
and leave those whom Allāh has created for you to be your
mates?
Indeed, you are a people transgressing (all limits).
{Al-Qur'an, 26: 165–166}

And (remember) Lot when he said to his people:
"Do you commit indecency (great sin, sodomy etc.) with your
eyes open?
Do you approach men lustfully instead of women?
No, you are a people who behave senselessly." {Al-Qur'an, 27: 54–55}

*Prophet Muḥammad ﷺ said: "If you find anyone doing as Lot's
people did (i.e. homosexual sodomy), kill the one who does it,
and the one to whom it is done." {Abū Dāwūd, Ḥadīth 4447. The Hadith
Software Version 1.0}*

These verses refer to the society of Lot (Lūṭ, peace be upon him). Allāh sent Lot to warn his people of the evil of their ways. They ignored these warnings. Eventually Allāh commanded Lot to leave with his family, whereafter He destroyed the whole town and all its inhabitants, because of their homosexual practices. Muslim jurists have held differing opinions concerning the punishment for this abominable practice, some stating the punishment for fornication, while some stating the death penalty for both the active and passive participants. It is important to mention that these rulings are not given in an anarchic sense where a Muslim takes the law into his own hands. Rather for these punishments to be implemented, due legal process needs to be carried out, which can only be done under a state implementing Islamic Law. While such punishments may seem cruel, they have been suggested to maintain the purity of the society and to keep it clean of perverted elements, allowing for the spiritual development of its members in an ideal environment. The spread of this depraved practice in a society disrupts its natural life pattern and makes those who practice it slaves to their lusts, depriving them of decent taste, decent morals, and a decent manner of living.

The institution of family is crucially important in Islām, and the rules governing interaction between the sexes are there to prevent harmful acts such as fornication and adultery. As we have said, outside of the immediate family, men and women must dress modestly, according to Islāmic guidelines. Free mixing is strongly discouraged, this all helps to prevent forbidden relationships.

Homosexuality presents a problem. It is not suggested that men will not mix with each other, nor that women will not mix with each other; they can do so within the limits set by the *Qur'ān* and the *Sunnah* of Prophet Muḥammad ﷺ. Those who seek to fulfil homosexual desires necessarily damage the very fabric of society which is why Islām condemns such practices.

It is worth commenting on the terms 'homophobia' and 'heterosexism'. Homophobia generally means a fear of homosexuals or homosexuality. The Islāmic viewpoint is not homophobic; disapproval is different from fear. Heterosexism has been defined as heterosexuals believing they are superior which justifies imposing values. In Islām it is not a question of superiority or inferiority, but one of right or wrong, in the same way that Islām says that theft is wrong or that murder is wrong.

Whilst Islām forbids homosexual practices, it does not seek out those with homosexual desires with a view to persecute them. If people have such desires, they should keep them to themselves, and should control their desires to avoid forbidden practices. The advice would be the same as, say, to someone who had sexual desires for minors or for close family: that having the desires does not legitimise realising them. Islām aims at closing all avenues that might encourage evil practice which could corrupt and pollute the whole society.

Jihād

Fight in the cause of *Allāh* those who fight you,
but do not transgress limits;
for *Allāh* loves not transgressors.
And slay them wherever you catch them,
and turn them out from where they have turned you out;
for tumult and oppression are worse than slaughter;
but fight them not at the Sacred Mosque [*Ka'bah*],
unless they (first) fight you there;
but if they fight you, slay them.
Such is the reward of those who suppress faith.
But if they cease, *Allāh* is Oft-Forgiving, Most Merciful.
And fight them on
until there is no more tumult or oppression,
and there prevail justice and faith in *Allāh*;
but if they cease,
let there be no hostility

except to those who practise oppression. *{Al-Qur'ān, chapter 2, verses 190-193}*

Of all the precepts of Islām, it is perhaps *Jihād* that is most often misquoted, misused and misunderstood. The word itself means 'to strive or struggle in the way of *Allāh*', not the more popular but incorrect usage, 'holy war'. A person striving in the way of *Allāh*, i.e. performing *Jihād*, is a *Mujāhid* (pl. *Mujāhidūn*).

Of course, a 'struggle in the way of *Allāh*' may mean warfare, but any personal or communal struggle to establish an Islāmic lifestyle is *Jihād*. In the warfare sense, *Jihād* is permitted in self-defence and to fight against oppression. The *Qur'ān* and the *Sunnah* (example) of Prophet Muḥammad ﷺ are explicit about not only *when* war is permissible but also *how* it is to be conducted, pre-dating the Geneva Conventions on war, prisoners-of-war and human rights by about 1300 years.

Nuclear bombs and other weapons which kill and maim indiscriminately are abhorrent to Islāmic concepts because it is inevitable that innocent people will suffer by their use. Non-combatants are to be spared, as is the environment; not even trees should be cut down in war if at all possible.

There is no such thing, therefore, as 'holy war' but there is 'just war' to establish justice, in self-defence and to protect one's life, family, home, etc. Islām demands that oppression be banished and if that requires fighting – *Jihād* – at whatever level (fighting for one's rights in civil life, for example), then so be it.

At the dawn of the third Christian millennium it is worth considering the cultural *Jihād* engaged in by Muslims around the world. Global communications beam anti-Islāmic images and messages into Muslim homes and the resultant erosion of Islāmic values is painfully obvious. There is a growing awareness of the cultural heritage of Islām and Muslims and its superiority over much of what today passes as culture in non-Muslim society. Serious efforts are being made to provide a viable and vibrant counter-culture to that presented as the norm by the Western media (and frequently aped by the Muslim media). This struggle is another manifestation of the real meaning of *Jihād*.

Marriage

O mankind, reverence your Guardian-Lord
Who created you from a single person,
created, of like nature, his mate,
and from them both scattered (like seeds)
countless men and women –

fear *Allah*,
through whom you demand your mutual rights,
and reverence the wombs that bore you:
for *Allah* ever watches over you. {*Al-Qur'an, chapter 4, verse 1*}

Marriage in Islam is a legally-binding agreement between a man and a woman establishing their intention and mutual commitment to live together according to the teachings of the faith. They must remember their duty to *Allah* and to each other at all times, and that they have mutual rights and responsibilities.

The selection of marriage partners between Muslims is often regarded as old-fashioned by non-Muslims. Because Islam emphasises chastity and modesty, there is normally very little social contact between young Muslim men and women, especially of the kind which is regarded as perfectly normal in non-Muslim society. For practising Muslims there is no such thing as dating or premarital intimacy of any kind. In Islam, sexual behaviour and acts are only for those legally within the security of a marriage. There should be no sexual experimentation before marriage and fidelity within marriage is essential.

Although young people are at liberty to express their preferences and state what they are looking for in a prospective partner, it is not the usual practice for them actively to seek a partner for themselves. This is mostly done by their parents, or other elders within the family. In other words, it is usually an 'arranged marriage'. Arranged marriages must fulfil the basic condition of the freely given consent of both the bride and the groom. A 'forced' marriage, where consent has not been given by either the bride or groom, or is given only under excessive pressure, is a different matter; this would be contrary to the teachings of Islam, and would immediately call into question the validity of the marriage. Some Muslim parents do place undue pressure on their children, especially their daughters, in the choice of partner for marriage; in particular, they may place greater emphasis on 'family honour' than on the welfare and happiness of their children. It is a practice that should not be continued. Open and frank discussion about marriage between parents and their children would help avoid misunderstandings and unreasonable exercise of parental authority.

Arranged marriages, then, are the general custom amongst Muslims as the best way to find, vet and meet potential husbands or wives within the overall context of the Islamic way of life. Once a potential match is arranged, the most important Islamic requirement is the freely given consent of both the prospective bride and groom; without this, the marriage should not proceed. Arranged marriages are not, of course, unique to Muslims; other religious groups use similar matchmaking methods and such marriages are generally more stable and less prone to divorce than marriages based on premarital emotional and sexual experimentation or experience.

The main quality to look for in a potential partner in marriage has been given by Prophet Muḥammad ﷺ:

> *"A woman is married for four things: her wealth, her family status, her beauty and her religion. So you should marry the religious woman (otherwise) you will be a loser."*
> *{Al-Bukhārī}*

> *"Do not marry only for the sake of beauty, as perhaps the beauty will become the cause of moral decline. Do not marry even for the sake of wealth, as perhaps the wealth will become the reason for disobedience. Marry rather on the grounds of religious devotion."* *{Ibn Mājah}*

The other vital part of a marriage agreement is the *mahr* (dowry) which is paid by the man to the woman (not the reverse as in some other cultures) and is for the use of the woman alone unless she decides otherwise. This can be cash, jewellery or even something simple such as a copy of the *Qur'ān*. It is against the spirit and intention behind the *mahr* for it to be set at such an exorbitant rate that poor people can't afford to marry.

Islām recognises that there are physical and mental differences between men and women. Husbands and wives are companions for each other, and they have clearly defined roles within the family. The husband is responsible for the economic maintenance of the family, and the wife is responsible for the management of the household affairs. The family responsibilities are shared between them. Islām recognises the leadership of men over women, but it does not recognise the domination of one over the other. Even if her wealth is greater than her husband's, the wife is under no obligation to maintain the family financially, although, of course, she may if she wishes. She should support her husband at all times unless he specifically asks her to disobey *Allāh*. The husband must be considerate towards his wife and concerned for her welfare. At all times, both husband and wife must reserve their sexuality exclusively for each other.

A Muslim woman, married or single, is a person in her own right; she is not merely an adjunct to her husband, father or brothers. Islāmic law preceded modern Western law by thirteen centuries in granting women the right to own property and have their own earnings (even after marriage), something she can share with her husband or not; the decision is hers. The stereotype image of Muslim women as servants forever in the house cooking and cleaning, with no spirituality, personality, interests or personal life, has no basis in Islāmic teachings. Men and women are completely equal in terms of accountability to *Allāh*. However, equal doesn't mean 'the same' – physical differences and capabilities alone should demonstrate that – but both have the same religious obligations and, if *Allāh* wills it, the same rewards in this life and in the Hereafter.

It is common for critics of Islām to try to 'prove' that Islām does not treat men and women equally by quoting the inheritance laws, by which men inherit a greater share of an estate than women. But if we consider the point mentioned earlier about the responsibility men have of looking after the women in their household, it should be clear that a larger inheritance helps to defray such an additional financial burden. What the women don't get as a direct legacy, they get indirectly through the inheritance of the male responsible for their upkeep.

There are many sayings of Prophet Muḥammad ﷺ that entreat men to show kindness and consideration for women. Muslim men should always show great respect, honour and tenderness to their wives.

Both men and women have the freedom to contribute to society in keeping with their own particular skills and interests, providing they maintain their personal dignity and modesty, and keep within the limits set by Islām. Women can fulfil many essential roles in society (e.g. in education, medicine and social work); at the time of the Prophet ﷺ women were active in the struggle against paganism. Prophet Muḥammad's wives (may *Allāh* be pleased with them) were consulted by many people (men and women); among them, 'Ā'ishah was an expert on the sayings of the Prophet ﷺ and Islāmic jurisprudence.

The tone for the marriage relationship is set by *Allāh* in the *Qur'ān*:

And among His signs is this, that He created for you mates from among yourselves, that you may dwell in tranquillity with them and He has put love and mercy between your hearts: verily in that are signs for those who reflect. *{Al-Qur'ān, chapter 30, verse 21}*

Thus, there should be mutual respect, kindness, love, companionship and harmonious interaction between husband and wife.

Although, in practice, women generally do the domestic work in a Muslim home, this is not a legal (Islāmic law) requirement; it usually stems from the respective working roles of the husband and wife, one outside the home (usually, but not necessarily, the husband), the other within the home, looking after any children. Men should, however, help their wives in household chores, following the example of the Prophet ﷺ who helped his wives and mended his own clothes when the need arose.

In a Muslim marriage, both husband and wife have a responsibility to meet one another's sexual needs. There should be no extramarital sexual activity for married Muslims (or, as stated earlier, premarital intimacy for unmarried Muslims). Adultery and fornication are not only serious sins but also – in Islāmic law – serious crimes with severe punishments. The reason is obvious when you look at the disruption to family life and society in general as a result of adulterous behaviour.

> **The woman and the man guilty of adultery or fornication,
> flog each of them with a hundred stripes. Let not compassion
> move you in their case, in a matter prescribed by *Allāb*, if you
> believe in *Allāb* and the last day. And let a party of the believers
> witness the punishment.** *{Al-Qur'ān, chapter 24, verse 2}*

Any act that destabilises marriage will also destabilise society. Hence, the Islāmic punishments for such acts are severe. The punishments for fornication and adultery (*Zinā*) fall within prescribed limits (*Ḥudūd*, sing. *Ḥadd*), which cannot be changed and should be enforced according to Islāmic law in an Islāmic society. [*see also* CAPITAL PUNISHMENT]

The punishment for fornication and sodomy is one hundred lashes. Married men and women found guilty of adultery are to be stoned to death. A rapist incurs the same punishment as a married adulterer. Prophet Muḥammad ﷺ said:

> *When an unmarried male commits fornication with an
> unmarried female, they should receive one hundred lashes and
> exile for one year. And in the case of a married male
> committing adultery with a married female, they shall receive
> one hundred lashes and be stoned to death.* {Muslim}

The punishment when someone falsely accuses another of fornication or adultery (*Qadhf*) is eighty lashes and the permanent ineligibility of being a witness in a court of law.

> **And those who launch a charge against chaste women,
> and produce not four witnesses
> (to support their allegations),
> flog them with eighty stripes;
> and reject their evidence ever after:
> for such men are wicked transgressors.
> Unless they repent thereafter and mend (their conduct);
> for *Allāb* is Oft-Forgiving, Most Merciful.**

And for those who launch a charge against their spouses,
and have (in support) no evidence but their own,
their solitary evidence (can be received)
if they bear witness four times (with an oath) by *Allāh*
that they are solemnly telling the truth;
and the fifth (oath) (should be)
that they solemnly invoke
the curse of *Allāh* on themselves
if they tell a lie.
But it would avert the punishment from the wife,
if she bears witness four times (with an oath) by *Allāh*,
that (her husband) is telling a lie;
and the fifth (oath) should be
that she solemnly invokes the wrath of *Allāh* on herself
if (her accuser) is telling the truth.
If it were not for *Allāh's* grace and mercy on you,
and that *Allāh* is Oft-Returning, full of Wisdom,
(You would be ruined indeed). *{Al-Qur'ān, chapter 24, verses 4–10}*

The Prophet ﷺ discouraged anything that might lead to promiscuity, saying:

The Zina of the eye is the look,
the Zinā of the tongue is the word;
the Zinā of the foot is walking towards the desires. {Abū Dāwūd}

It is interesting to note *Biblical* sayings on this subject:

You shall not commit adultery. {Exodus 20:14}

When a man is discovered lying with a married woman,
they shall both die,
the woman as well as the man who lay with her,
you shall rid Israel of this wickedness.
When a virgin is pledged in marriage to a man
and another man comes upon her in the town and lies with her,
you shall bring both of them out to the gate of that town
and stone both of them to death;
the girl because, although in the town, she did not cry for help,
and the man because he dishonoured another man's wife;
you shall rid yourselves of this wickedness. {Deuteronomy 22:22-24}

Do not commit adultery... {Matthew 19:18, Mark 10:19, Luke 18:20}

Islām, as a comprehensive way of life that builds community life on the basis of giving all people the opportunity to be part of a stable and caring family structure, has allowed limited polygamy. There may be widows (particularly in times of war) or divorced women with children to look after for whom the possibility of finding unmarried men to marry is remote. By allowing limited polygamy, Islām ensures that such women are not destined to struggle in life as 'one-parent' families and offers the chance of a secure home again with all the rights of a wife. If a woman is unable to satisfy the sexual or other needs of her husband he may consider taking another wife, rather than the common Western practice of secretly taking a mistress. However, there are strict conditions laid down in the *Qur'ān* for this allowance: the husband must try to look after his wives equally in every respect, something the *Qur'ān* points out is not possible to do fully; he must also maintain them independently, in separate homes (not under the same roof), dividing his time equally between them. Polygyny (having more than one wife at the same time) was actually limited by Islām to four wives, there previously being no limit to the number of wives a man could have at any one time. Polyandry (having more than one husband at the same time) is forbidden in Islām; one reason for this is that in a society where inheritance and the laws relating to the persons eligible to marry one another are important, it is vital to know who the father of a particular child is; if a woman has more than one husband at any one time, such a distinction could be almost impossible to prove, even using the latest medical techniques such as DNA testing.

Unlike non-Muslim marriages in the West, where premarital love and intimacy are considered to be almost indispensable, the basic ingredient for a successful Muslim marriage is a shared set of values upon which to build a life together. A firm shared belief in Islām can often bind couples together in their relationship which can then withstand many of the pressures which force non-Muslim couples apart.

A Muslim marriage is seen as a very real relationship between two individuals who will not be 100% immune from the stress and strain of everyday life. However, their shared faith will help to cushion a Muslim couple from the worst effects of such things. Nevertheless, Islām is a very practical way of life and is realistic enough to prepare couples for the possibility that they might not be able to carry on together as husband and wife, for a variety of reasons, and so divorce – although hated – is allowed when all conciliatory efforts have failed. It is essential that a marriage should be harmonious and not injurious to the life and health of the couple and their families and, ultimately, society at large. [*see also* PARENTS AND CHILDREN, DIVORCE]

Music

Music is as much an emotive subject as it is a means to stir the emotions. The religion of Islām guides every aspect of a Muslim's life, so it is only reasonable that it should influence Muslim attitudes to music. Muslims are generally in agreement that there have to be some restrictions on music – few could advocate 'anything goes'. But amongst Muslims it has not always been clear exactly where to draw the line.

When looking at this issue we must consider: the effects of the music itself on people; the nature of any words set to the music; and activities linked with the music. Certain types of music clearly go against Islāmic teaching of morality, or even against the basic beliefs. For instance, some music, particularly many modern pop songs, accompanies sexually explicit lyrics. So-called 'death metal' music often contains Satanic references.

What is often referred to as 'classical' music (i.e. music for full or chamber orchestra, or ensembles made up of instrumentalists from such groups) may superficially appear less controversial. However, the overture *Romeo and Juliet* by Tchaikovsky or any one of a number of 'boy meets girl' operas (e.g. *Carmen* by Bizet) portray concepts that are alien to Islāmic beliefs (i.e. premarital intimacy). Sacred works, such as Vivaldi's *Gloria*, promote Trinitarian Christian beliefs, again in contradiction to Islāmic teachings.

Much modern music is made for dancing; young people of both sexes are encouraged to dance together, often intimately and suggestively. For the last few decades rock and pop music has been linked with the 'drug culture', the most recent manifestation of which is the taking of Ecstasy to 'enhance' the experience of 'raving'.

How should Muslims decide what sorts of music are acceptable? Whenever someone sets out to participate in a particular activity, they should first ascertain whether or not it is something that will contribute positively to their life. In Islam, this means whether it will make them more aware of their Creator and their role in life, or if it will divert them from the remembrance of *Allāh* and the Guidance He has given to mankind through His final Prophet, Muḥammad ﷺ.

To discover what is *ḥalāl* (permissible) or *ḥarām* (forbidden), Muslims turn to the *Qur'ān* and the *Sunnah*. As in all matters, our attitude when doing this is to determine what is correct and approved of, whether or not it coincides with our desires or understanding. Admittedly, it is sometimes difficult to prevent our judgement from being clouded by what we would wish to be true. This is especially the case with music, as music by its nature often has a unique hold on our emotions and spirit.

One verse of the *Qur'ān* often quoted when discussing this issue reads as follows:

> **And there are among men those who purchase idle talk**
> **in order to mislead others from *Allāh's* path without knowledge,**
> **and who throw ridicule upon it. For such there will be a**
> **humiliating punishment.** *{Al-Qur'ān, Chapter 31, verse 6}*

The phrase 'idle talk' has been described by commentators as 'anything which distracts and diverts one from *Allāh's* path'; however, although modern music in particular could most certainly be said to fit into that category, it is generally accepted that the verse in itself does not constitute a prohibition of music.

Turning to the second source of Islāmic law, the authentic *Sunnah* (example) of Prophet Muḥammad ﷺ, we see that in the most famous and authentic collection of the Prophet's sayings (*Aḥādīth*), the Prophet ﷺ is reported to have said:

> *"There will be [at some future time]*
> *people from my Ummah [nation]*
> *who will seek to make lawful*
> *fornication,*
> *the wearing of silk [for men],*
> *wine-drinking*
> *and the use of musical instruments..."* *{Al-Bukhārī}*

The fact that the Prophet ﷺ said "... will seek to make lawful... the use of musical instruments..." makes it clear that their use is, in fact, unlawful. The word translated as 'musical instruments', *ma'āzif*, has been clearly established – according to the correct Arabic usage – to mean (a) musical instruments, (b) the sounds of those musical instruments, and (c) singing to musical accompaniment. It does not include natural sounds, such as birdsong, even though such sounds are 'musical'. Nor does it include the unaccompanied human voice; normal speech, the call to prayer and the reciting of the Qur'ān cannot be described by the term *ma'āzif*. The general rule, then, is that most forms of music are prohibited, and this is reflected in what is known about the life of the Prophet ﷺ and his companions, and from the rulings given on this issue by some of the great Muslim scholars from the early days of Islām. However, looking further into the matter reveals that beyond the general prohibition there are certain exceptions.

At the time of Prophet Muḥammad ﷺ, his wife 'Ā'ishah had two girls with her who were playing on a hand drum and singing. The Prophet was also present, listening to them with his head under a shawl. 'Ā'ishah's father, Abū Bakr, came in and scolded the girls but the Prophet ﷺ uncovered his face and said, "Let them be, Abū Bakr, these are the days of *'Īd*." {Al-Bukhārī, Muslim}

From this we see that although Abū Bakr understood that music in general is *ḥarām*, the Prophet ﷺ wished to indicate that the celebration of *'Īd* is an exception. Thus singing and the use of a drum is not only permissible but recommended on days of celebration such as the two *'Īd* festivals and weddings. The condition stands, of course, that the singing and what accompanies it (i.e. the place and circumstances) must not be obscene or harmful to Islāmic standards of morality. Hence, unaccompanied songs about the love of *Allāh* and His prophets, the purpose of human life, the well-being of society and the appreciation of the beauty of nature are encouraged.

However, any activity that leads to, suggests or encourages behaviour, talk or discussion contrary to the teachings of Islām is considered to be in itself *ḥarām*. In short, the rule of thumb is "whatever leads to that which is *ḥarām* is itself *ḥarām*." It follows from this that it is prohibited for Muslims to listen to, or be otherwise involved with, most modern popular music or songs. Even if the subject matter of a song is *ḥalāl*, the manner in which it is sung, e.g. by the singer using suggestive sexual movements, may render the song itself *ḥarām*. In addition, if the singing is done in conjunction with *ḥarām* activities, such as in a disco, or a drinks party or suchlike, it is *ḥarām*.

It is clear, then, that the use of musical instruments *generally* is not allowed, and this has always been the view of the majority of Islāmic scholars. The fact that there are quite a few famous Muslim musicians who do not follow Islāmic guidance on this matter does not alter the Islāmic point of view.

It is true to say that in drawing the line as to what is allowed and what is not, inevitably there will be grey areas. The Prophet ﷺ said:

> *That which is lawful is plain*
> *and that which is unlawful is plain*
> *and between the two of them are doubtful matters*
> *about which not many people know.*
> *Thus he who avoids doubtful matters*
> *clears himself in regard to his religion and his honour...*
> {Al-Bukhārī, Muslim}

Life without music can be just as full and rich as life with music. *Allāh* has given us plenty of lawful and worthwhile pastimes. Many people who felt music to be an indispensable part of their lives have found, after abandoning it for the sake of *Allāh*, that this is certainly not the case.

Muslim Schools

It is arguable whether Church of England plans to expand the number of church-run schools in the 21st century would have ever seen the light of day if not for the growth of the Muslim schools' sector in Britain. Despite the existence, since 1998, of a handful of full-time state-funded Muslim schools, they remain a controversial subject. So much so, that in the wake of the riots in the north of England in 2001, the Home office report, chaired by Ted Cantle, appeared to lay the blame for the lack of "integration" and thus the blame for the riots themselves on faith schools. The Cantle Rport calmly overlooked the fact that the rioters in Bradford, for example, would have attended ordinary state schools, not Muslim boys' schools, because the latter do not exist in that city. The problems arose, therefore, out of an inadequate state system, not the presence of faith schools.

Such demonisation of Muslim schools challenges people to examine their own levels of acceptance and understanding of Islam and Muslims and, indeed, has led to a growing examination of the nature of British multi-cultural approaches to the education of our children.

Supporters of Cantle's conclusions suggest that Muslim schools are divisive at a time when "community cohesion" is the latest buzz phrase. Muslim children attending schools with an Islamic ethos will not, the argument runs, be capable of living as British citizens in any meaningful way. The evidence suggests otherwise. Ex-pupils of Muslim schools, which have been around for almost 25 years now, are to be found in all walks of life, having gone through the system and emerged at the other end as young Muslim adults confident enough in their identity and self-esteem to play a full and active role at university and the work-place. They have not, and do not, live in a vacuum, especially in this internet age. The state-funding of Muslim schools in some areas, and the increasing acknowledgement by the authorities that those which wish to stay independent are fulfilling a crucial function, has created a more open and accepting arena within which Muslim children are educated. Recognising that Muslim parents who opt for faith schools built around Islam also have valid aspirations for their children, is one way that local education authorities have sought to widen the options available in terms of parental choice, a concept that has been a cornerstone of education since 1944.

Although some critics of Muslim schools accuse them of being 'Asian' enclaves, the schools themselves, of course, simply reflect the communities they serve, much as the local non-faith state schools do. If a school is situated in a predominantly 'Asian' area, the pupils will be nearly all from an 'Asian' background. Schools in all-white areas also reflect the make-up of the local community. Muslim schools are no exception, although with the relatively recent migration of Muslim communities from around the Middle East, North and East Africa, Muslim schools are increasingly multi-racial in their intake. This is true, also, of the staff at these schools, but despite the multi-racial and often multicultural nature of Muslim schools, one thing binds staff and pupils together: the common belief in Islam, a faith for all people, regardless of race.

In the eighties, the initial development of Muslim schools tended to be either at a primary level or for girls only at the secondary stage. The reasons for this largely revolved around two issues: cost and the perceived desire to protect girls who were regarded as being more vulnerable and open to abuse due to the distinctive nature of their dress requirements. The dispute over and banning of the Hijab in French schools indicates that nothing much has changed over the intervening years, at least across the channel and among opponents of Muslim schools who cite the "common sense approach" of the French authorities towards "blatant religious symbols" in supposedly "secular" schools. In a democracy this is itself a discriminatory argument: girls in Muslim schools do not suffer from the kind of discrimination and abuse that many face in non-faith schools; their academic progress benefits as a result. On a wider front, it is generally accepted that girls perform better and achieve higher grades in single-sex schools, at least up to the age of sixteen. Annual league tables regularly show single-sex schools at the top, for boys and girls.

The demand that schools should be strictly secular in nature, and claims that secularism is "neutral" form part of the effort to remove religion from public life and that, for believers of any faith, not least the Muslims, is simply unacceptable. A conscious decision not to practise, or to prevent others from practising, a religion is never a neutral position to take. Arguments against faith schools based on this premise, far from sounding rational and reasonable actually demonstrate a degree of compulsion of the kind proponents claim to find abhorrent in faith schools. The paradox is clear.

Faith schools, and Muslim schools in particular, form a vibrant part of the overall education provision in Britain that allows for parental choice and a degree of religious pluralism that speaks well of traditional British values. A growing number of Muslim schools, state-funded and independent, are developing an enviable track record of academic success across the Key Stages, as well as an Islamic ethos that nurtures young people in the faith of their community, preparing them for life in a wider society that is increasingly challenging to people of all faiths and none. That is the aim of all education and, as more and more Muslims begin to see the benefits of full-time Islamic education for their children, places at Muslim schools are in great demand. Parents are aware that the dreams of returning one day to their places of origin, dreams held by themselves and their own parents and grandparents, no longer hold anything of value for their children, and that they must prepare them for life in this country. That alone is a wonderful incentive for Muslim schools to be at the cutting edge of educational development, to ensure that their pupils are more than capable of facing life in the global village that is today's world. It is a challenge that Muslim schools are embracing with enthusiasm, attracting many more supporters in the process.

Parents and Children

Islām puts great emphasis on the importance of the family. The basis of this is Islāmic marriage [see MARRIAGE], but also important is the relationship between parents and children. There are many verses of the *Qur'ān* and *Aḥādīth* that underline this. The following is a small selection:

> **And We made it a duty for man**
> **to be good to his parents.**
> **His mother bears him**
> **with one fainting spell after another,**
> **while his weaning takes two years.**
> **Thank Me as well as your parents;**
> **towards Me lies the goal.** *{Al-Qur'ān, chapter 31, verse 14}*

> **Be kind to your parents and relatives,**
> **and to orphans and those in need;**
> **and speak nicely to people.** *{Al-Qur'ān, chapter 2, verse 83}*

> **Your Lord has ordered that you worship none but Him**
> **and (show) kindness to your parents,**
> **whether either of them or both of them attain old age in life,**
> **never say to them "ugh!" nor be harsh to them,**
> **but speak to them kindly.**
> **And serve them with tenderness and humility and say,**
> **"My Lord, have mercy on them,**
> **just as they cared for me as a little child."** *{Al-Qur'ān, chapter 17, verses 23-24}*

> **O you who believe! Save yourselves and your families**
> **from a Fire whose fuel is people and stones.** *{Al-Qur'ān, chapter 66, verse 6}*

'Abdullāh ibn Ma'sūd said, "I asked the Prophet ﷺ which action Allāh, the Mighty and Exalted, loves best? He said, 'Prayer at its proper time.' I asked, 'And after that?' He said, 'Then kindness to parents.' I asked, 'And after that?' He said, 'Then Jihād in the way of Allāh.'" {Al-Bukhārī}

A man asked Prophet Muhammad ﷺ, "O Messenger of Allāh! Who deserves the best care from me?" The Prophet ﷺ said, "Your mother." The man asked, "Who then?" The Prophet ﷺ said, "Your mother." The man asked yet again, "Who then?" Prophet Muhammad ﷺ said, "Your mother." The man asked once more, "Who then?" The Prophet ﷺ then said, "Your father." {Al-Bukhārī}

A man came to the Prophet ﷺ and said, "Messenger of Allāh, I desire to go on a military expedition and I have come to consult you." He ﷺ asked him if he had a mother, and when he replied that he had, he said, "Stay with her, for Paradise is at her feet." {An-Nasā'ī}

The Prophet ﷺ said, "He is not one of us who has no compassion for our little ones and does not honour our old ones." {At-Tirmidhī}

Prophet Muhammad ﷺ said, "No father can give his child anything better than good manners." {Al-Tirmidhī}

Prophet Muhammad ﷺ said, "Be careful of your duty to Allāh and be fair and just to your children." {Al-Bukhārī}

Prophet Muhammad ﷺ said, "Shall I tell you which is the worst of the great sins?" He repeated that three times. They replied, "Yes, Messenger of Allāh." He said, "Associating something else with Allāh and disobeying parents." He had been reclining, but then he sat up and said, "Beware of lying." {Al-Bukhārī}

Prophet Muhammad ﷺ said, "Three supplications are answered without a doubt: the supplication of someone who is oppressed, the supplication of someone who is on a journey and the supplication of parents for their children." {Al-Bukhārī}

Prophet Muḥammad ﷺ said, "When a person dies, all his actions come to an end with the exception of three things: continuing charity, knowledge that benefits, or a righteous child who makes supplication for him." {Al-Bukhārī}

Racism

And among His Signs
is the creation of the Heavens and the Earth,
and the variations in your languages and your colours;
verily, in that there are Signs for those who know. *{Al-Qur'ān, chapter 30, verse 22}*

O mankind,
We created you from a single pair
of a male and a female,
and made you into tribes and nations
that you may know each other
(not that you despise each other).
Verily, the most honoured of you
in the sight of *Allāh*
is he who is the most righteous of you... *{Al-Qur'ān, chapter 49, verse 13}*

Racism, whether open or hidden, is an evil aspect of life which Islām seeks to eradicate. It is clear from verses in the *Qur'ān* and some of the sayings of Prophet Muḥammad ﷺ that differences in colour, tribe, race or traditions are not to be used as excuses for unjust treatment. [*see also* SLAVERY]

The *Ḥajj* – the annual pilgrimage to *Makkah* – is the prime example of the multiracial aspect of Islām: Muslims of all races gather with one common purpose – to worship *Allāh*. The equality of human beings in all matters except piety (which we are encouraged to try to increase) is clear. Under no circumstances can a person be ill-treated or abused simply because they happen to be of a different race. As you can gather, therefore, Muslims are not a distinct racial or ethnic group, to be classified by people as 'Asians' or 'Arabs' to the exclusion of the other races which all belong to the family of Islām.

The Islāmic message of universal brotherhood and equality made a profound impact on El-Hajj Malik El-Shabazz, who was better known as Malcolm X. Although his youth was characterised by crime and drugs, he turned his back on that life and became one of the most outspoken and charismatic speakers against the injustice and racism suffered by black people in the USA. However, he had come to believe that all 'whites' were evil and only 'blacks' were good. Although he considered himself a Muslim, he did not really know the teachings of Islām. Then, he took the opportunity to perform the *Ḥajj*, and this was to change his thinking forever:

> Never have I witnessed such sincere hospitality and the overwhelming spirit of true brotherhood as is practised by people of all colors and races here in this ancient Holy Land, the home of Abraham, Muhammad, and all the other prophets of the Holy Scriptures. For the past week, I have been utterly speechless and spellbound by the graciousness I see displayed all around me by people *of all colors....*

> There were tens of thousands of pilgrims, from all over the world. They were of all colours, from blue-eyed blonds to black-skinned Africans. But we were all participating in the same ritual, displaying a spirit of unity and brotherhood that my experiences in America had led me to believe never could exist between the white and non-white.

> America needs to understand Islam, because this is the one religion that erases from its society the race problem. Throughout my travels in the Muslim world, I have met, talked to, and even eaten with people who in America would have been considered 'white' – but the 'white' attitude was removed from their minds by the religion of Islam. I have never before seen *sincere* and *true* brotherhood practiced by all colors together, irrespective of their color.

> You may be shocked by these words coming from me. But on this pilgrimage, what I have seen, and experienced, has forced me to *re-arrange* much of my thought-patterns previously held, and to *toss aside* some of my previous conclusions. This was not too difficult for me. Despite my firm convictions, I have been always a man who tries to face facts, and to accept the reality of life as new experience and knew knowledge unfolds it. I have always kept an open mind, which is necessary to the flexibility that must go hand in hand with every form of intelligent search for truth.

> During the past eleven days in the Muslim world, I have eaten from the same plate, drunk from the same glass, and slept in the same bed (or on the same rug) – while praying to the *same God* – with fellow Muslims, whose eyes were the bluest of blue, whose hair was the blondest of blond, and whose skin was the whitest of white. And in the *words* and in the *actions* and in the *deeds* of the 'white' Muslims, I felt the same sincerity that I felt among the black African Muslims of Nigeria, Sudan and Ghana.

> We were truly all the same (brothers) – because their belief in one God had removed the 'white' from their *minds*, the 'white' from their *behaviour*, and the 'white' from their *attitude*.

> I could see from this, that perhaps if white Americans could accept the Oneness of God, then perhaps, too, they could accept *in reality* the Oneness of Man – and cease to measure, and hinder, and harm others in terms of their 'differences' in color.

{The Autobiography of Malcolm X}

Sexually Transmitted Diseases
(AIDS/HIV)

Promiscuity, both heterosexual and homosexual, leads to innumerable problems: for an Islāmic society, based as it is on family life, trust, fidelity, love and accountability to *Allāh*, promiscuous behaviour based solely on selfish physical gratification with little care for the ultimate consequences of one's actions is totally unacceptable. Apart from the break-ups of family relationships (with the resultant proliferation of single-parent families and the psychological effects on adults and children alike) such behaviour spreads both physical and mental diseases, a case in point being AIDS.

Of course, a cure must be found (*Allāh* willing) to help those unfortunate enough to be HIV positive (which may lead to 'full-blown' AIDS). Such efforts are a humanitarian necessity. However, while the medical scientists are trying to make a breakthrough in their search for a cure, Islām has some very positive and radical things to say about how the disease is caught and spread in the first place.

> *Prophet Muḥammad ﷺ said, "Every intoxicant is khamr and every khamr is Ḥarām [forbidden]."*
> {*Muslim Vol. 3, Ḥadīth 4963, 4964 & 4966 p.1108*}

> *Prophet Muḥammad ﷺ said, "If fornication should become widespread, you should realise that this has never happened without new diseases befalling the people which their forebears never suffered." {Ibn Mājah, Ḥadīth 4009. www.al-islam.com (Arabic)}*

> **Let those who find not the wherewithal for marriage keep themselves chaste until Allāh gives them the means out of His grace.** {Al-Qur'ān, chapter 24, verse 33}

HIV is mostly transmitted as a result of drug abuse, sexual promiscuity and homosexual acts, all forbidden in Islām. However, these days anyone who declares that homosexuality is a perverted way of life – as Muslims must – is accused of intolerance. Muslims believe, though, that such behaviour has been forbidden by *Allāh* (God) for very real reasons and if we ignore His guidance there are bound to be harmful effects on society. Tragically, HIV has now spread to the innocent through unfaithful husbands and wives, infected blood transfusions, as well as to children born to infected parents. If people had all followed the way of life of Islām, no one would have suffered and died from AIDS. By the end of 2003, 37 million adults and 2.5 million children were living with HIV in the world (according to estimates from the Joint United Nations Programme on HIV/AIDS (UNAIDS) and the World Health Organization (WHO), reported in *http://www.avert.org/worlstatinfo.htm,* last updated December 9, 2003).

Muslims believe that sex education should give clear warnings, and discourage sexual experimentation before marriage. The advice usually offered to people (especially young people), in the efforts to prevent sexually transmitted diseases (STDs) without 'spoiling sexual enjoyment', frequently overlooks the doubtful advisability and morality of casual sexual liaisons. Instead of assuming that because some people are sexually active at a young age all young people must be given as much information and contraceptive advice as possible, more attention should be paid to getting the message across that 'No sex outside marriage' is the most effective form of protection from sexually transmitted diseases.

The concept of what constitutes 'acceptable' behaviour in society needs to be redefined. It is often said that if you want to know the future, look into the past: history shows that some civilisations collapsed once homosexuality was tolerated as normal behaviour. Sadly, in this secular world, the guidance given by *Allāh* is rejected more often than not. It is shocking for Muslim parents to read that "Only 3 per cent of young people [aged 16 – 24] believe that sexual intercourse should be reserved for marriage, with nearly half admitting to their first experience before the age of 16..." (*The Independent,* 21 July 1992).

A stable, responsible and caring society is only possible where sexual relationships are based on heterosexual marriage; there should be no place for extramarital affairs and deviant practices such as homosexuality.

Slavery

But he [Man] has made no haste
on the path that is steep
[the path of virtue].
And what will explain to you
the path that is steep?
(It is) the freeing of the bondman... {*Al-Qur'ān, chapter 90, verses 11-13*}

Abū Dharr narrated, "There was a quarrel between me and another man whose mother was a non-Arab, and I called her

> *bad names. The man complained about me to the Prophet* ﷺ. *The Prophet* ﷺ *said, 'Did you abuse so-and-so?' I said, 'Yes.' He said, 'Did you call his mother bad names?' I said, 'Yes.' He said, 'You still have the traits of (the pre-Islamic period of) ignorance.' I said, '(Do I still have ignorance) even now in my old age?'*
>
> *He said, 'Yes, they [slaves] are your brothers and Allāh has put them under your command. So the one under whose hand Allāh has put his brother, should feed him from what he eats, and clothe him in what he wears, and should not ask him to do anything beyond his capacity. And if ever he asks him to do a hard task, he should help him with it.'"* {Al-Bukhārī}

Slavery existed in non-Muslim societies all over the world at the time of Prophet Muḥammad ﷺ, including the pagan society of Arabia. Today we tend to think of the vile Atlantic slave trade when considering the subject, and we regard the British government's abolition of that trade in 1807 and of slavery itself in 1833 as the end of that chapter in history. However, slavery in all but name remains with us to this day around the globe. Economic slavery, child labour, cultural slavery and so on are reminders that slavery takes more than one form and that exploitation of anyone is an unnatural and inhuman act. Talk of 'equality' for everyone has little meaning whilst such travesties exist.

It was the fact that Islām preaches absolute equality between people (except in the matter of piety), regardless of their status in life (i.e. 'master' or 'slave') which provoked the wrath of the pagans in *Makkah* against the Prophet ﷺ. It also made the faith very attractive to the poorer sections of the community and, in fact, many of the early Muslims were slaves.

Allāh declares in the *Qur'ān* that the freeing of a slave (… *'bondman'*…) is a virtuous act. The sayings of Prophet Muḥammad ﷺ also make this clear. The two combined (*Qur'ān* and the *Aḥādīth*) emphasise that slaves, if held, are to be fed and clothed like their owners and given rights as human beings which had previously been denied. For example, they could marry and could not be separated from their husband or wife; parents could not be separated from their children, and so on. This, of course, enraged slave-owners and made it almost impossible for the master/slave relationship to continue. Muslims, therefore, saw freeing slaves as a means to please *Allāh* and His Prophet.

The Prophet ﷺ said, "Whoever frees a Muslim slave, Allāh will save all the parts of his body from the (Hell) Fire as he has freed the body-parts of the slave." {Al-Bukhāri}

Sincerely practising Muslims, therefore, will not adhere to slavery because the example of Prophet Muḥammad ﷺ and his companions was to the contrary. The practice of Islām in this respect thus leads to a *de facto* prohibition of slavery in all forms. [*see also* RACISM]

Suicide

O you who believe!
Seek help with patient perseverance and prayer:
for Allāh is with those who patiently persevere.
And do not say of those who are slain in the way of Allāh:

"They are dead." Nay, they are they are living,
though you do not perceive (it)

Be sure that We shall test you
with something of fear and hunger,
some loss in goods or lives
or the fruits (of your toil),
but give glad tidings
to those who patiently persevere;
who say, when afflicted with calamity,
"To Allāh we belong and to Him is our return." *{Al-Qur'ān, chapter 2, verses 153-156}*

Muslims believe that every soul has been created by *Allāh*, a soul and a life which *Allāh* has made sacred. To kill anyone unlawfully is a great sin. Likewise, to kill oneself is forbidden. We did not create ourselves so we have no right to end our life. To look after yourself (and others) is a trust given to mankind by *Allāh*. This is made clear in the *Qur'ān*:

... nor kill (or destroy) yourselves;
indeed, Allāh has been most merciful to you. *{Al-Qur'ān, chapter 4, verse 29}*

A Muslim is taught to face hardships and pain with patience in the knowledge that whatever happens in this life is but a test for the Day of Judgement; the real life is in the Hereafter. Hence, not even the worst calamities that may befall a person in this life should be considered to be so serious that a person is tempted to take his or her own life.

In addition to the above verse of the *Qur'ān*, Prophet Muḥammad ﷺ has warned that anyone who commits suicide will be deprived of *Allāh's* mercy on the Day of Judgement. He said,

> *"In the time before you, a man was wounded. His wounds troubled him so much that he took a knife and cut his wrist and bled himself to death. Thereupon Allāh said, 'My slave hurried in the matter of his life, therefore he is deprived of the Paradise.'"* {Al-Bukhārī, Muslim}

If someone is deprived of Paradise because he cannot bear the pain of his wounds, how serious is it for someone to kill themselves because of a material loss, in business for example? The following *ḥadīth* (saying) of the Prophet ﷺ should be a warning to those who think that their troubles and pain will cease by taking their own life:

> *"He who throws himself down from a (high) rock and commits suicide will be throwing himself into Hell; he who drinks poison and kills himself will have the poison in his hand, drinking it forever in the fire of Hell; and he who kills himself with a weapon will have that weapon in his hand, stabbing himself forever in the fire of Hell."* {Al-Bukhārī, Muslim}

The above would also apply to euthanasia, in which people consent to a third party ending their life 'painlessly', especially if they are suffering through some illness. Central to the Islāmic viewpoint on this issue is a firm belief in *Allāh*, the Day of Judgement (when we will have to account for our lives on this Earth) and life in the Hereafter.

Surrogacy

Surrogate motherhood is a new development in society arising as a result of the advances made in genetic engineering and the ability to fertilise an embryo and replant it in the womb.

It is clear from written materials available on this subject that such a development has been founded on a humanist, secular point of view. All reservations or moral questions raised relate, in the main, to social considerations. Even the legal considerations involved are based on man-made laws which are changeable to suit the social climate.

In Islām, family life is governed by laws taken directly from the *Qur'ān* and the *Sunnah* (the example of Prophet Muḥammad ﷺ), or from basic rules deduced from them. Hence, there are areas and topics where changes in those laws cannot even be contemplated.

No physical relationship is to be established between a man and a woman except within the framework of marriage, as set out in the Islāmic *Sharī'ah* (Law) which gives clear rules to be followed. Children from a marriage have the basic undeniable right of the fatherhood and the motherhood of the couple concerned. The Islāmic laws of inheritance and the rules guiding the prohibited degrees of marriage make it vital for the natural parentage to be absolutely clear.

No Muslim man is allowed to donate sperm to a woman who is not his legal wife and no woman is allowed to donate an egg to another woman. No child can be called after a person unless the sperm is that of the person to whom he belongs and he has been borne (and born) by the woman who is the legal wife of the man concerned.

If a woman bears a child of another woman the child belongs, legally, to the woman who actually carries and gives birth. The other woman has no claim whatsoever on the child.

The issue revolves around the question of how the woman who gives birth was actually impregnated: how was the embryo placed in her womb? If we are talking about a married couple where the wife is unable to have a child and the 'surrogate mother' has been artificially impregnated with the sperm of the husband, this is not legally acceptable; it is, in effect, adultery because the Muslim woman is only allowed to conceive within marriage with sperm from her own husband. (If a married woman conceives using sperm from a third party because her husband is infertile, this is also adulterous. 'Sperm banks' are thus illegal in Islāmic law.)

If a woman carries an embryo fertilised with the sperm and egg of another couple, the child legally belongs to the 'surrogate mother'. No one has the right to claim parentage of a child other than the woman who bears it and her husband. A saying of Prophet Muḥammad ﷺ is clear in this respect:

> *"The child belongs to the bed (i.e. where the married couple sleep, which means the existing marriage). And for the fornicator is the stone."* {Al-Bukhārī}

In other words, if someone claims to be the father of a child conceived by a married woman, the child legally belongs to the husband of the woman and the claimant is to be silenced and his claim rejected. As long as the husband of the 'surrogate mother' does not deny the fatherhood of the child, the child is legally his in all outward matters.

It should be kept in mind that in cases like this, judgements are subject to external proofs; judges do not have the ability to look into people's hearts. All they can do is look into such proofs and leave the rest to *Allāh*.

An unmarried woman is not allowed to bear children (hence, even if surrogacy was allowed in Islām, the 'surrogate mother' would herself have to be a married woman) unless she claims to have been raped and this crime is established. In such a case she will be saved from the punishment accorded to adulterers in Islāmic law and the child will carry her name, not that of the rapist.

It can be seen, therefore, that surrogacy breaches Islāmic law in more than one respect and throws up many illegal and immoral possibilities; hence, it is not legal in Islām. Anyone resorting to it is committing a great sin. The child belongs to the woman who bears him and can not legally be handed over to the 'real' mother. There should, therefore, be no surrogate motherhood in an Islāmic society. [*Prepared by the late Dr Syed M. Ad-Darsh*]

Terrorism

Terrorism is not something that Muslims would attribute to or link with Islam, although the current situation in the world makes it difficult to disassociate terrorism from the actions of some Muslims. However, the whole aspect of terrorism has to be put into context before we look at the perceived role of terrorism in Islam, or in the name of Islam or mischievously linked to Islam.

There are almost as many definitions of terrorism as there are dictionaries, but the one that is close to being a generally-held understanding is thus:

Terror(-ism): *Systematic violence carried out against private citizens, public property and political enemies with the aim of enforcing demands or maintaining supremacy; the use of terror, violence and intimidation, usually by an underground or revolutionary group but sometimes to achieve a political end.*

If we are objective in this matter, it becomes very clear that such a definition can be applied to many different nations, faith groups and ideologies. It doesn't take a great leap of faith to be able to apply this definition to the actions of nations and states that today use the word terrorists to describe groups of Muslims. Go one step further, and we can see that if we use the criteria applied by the United States of America to define what the administration calls 'rogue states' and examine the actions of the USA against those criteria, then, as both Noam Chomsky and William Blum claim, the greatest rogue state is the USA itself (See Chomsky's book *Rogue States – the rule of force in world affairs*, and Blum's book similarly titled, *Rogue State*.)

Looking at other nations at the forefront of the 'war on terrorism', that is, those nations pointing accusatory fingers at others and denouncing them as terrorists, we see Britain and Israel, two nations whose pasts and presents are steeped in acts which constitute terrorism no matter how it is defined. Britain has used force to maintain supremacy in any number of places around the world, from Southern Africa and India during the 19th century to Afghanistan and Iraq. Israel was founded on the terrorism of the Stern Gang and Irgun, terrorism directed at the British mandatory power in Palestine and against the Palestinian population. Zionist terror has continued to today with Israel's illegal 36 year military occupation of the West Bank and Gaza Strip.

Hence, before we even begin to link any religion with acts of terror, we need to look at who is defining who is a terrorist and what is terrorism. The world's "leaders" at the moment are in no position to act as judge, jury and executioner for others. There is, for example, any number of countries regarded today as models of "democratic values", that went through violent revolutions, wars or other acts which could easily be described as terrorism. The USA fought for independence against Britain, and then carried out a systematic genocide against the native population. Britain is a country with a long, bloody history of wars, both civil and external, acts of resistance and conquest by force. France and Russia had their own revolutions and each has a colonial history with a track record of oppression of the natives. The most startling example of the hypocrisy and double-standards used when defining who is and is not a terrorist is Nelson Mandela and the ANC. If the current anti-terrorism legislation had been in place a few years ago, it would have been illegal to have supported the ANC in the struggle against the evils of apartheid in South Africa. Margaret Thatcher famously called Mandela a terrorist and yet few today would disagree that he is one of the most respected politicians and elder statesmen on the world scene, as well as being the most recognisable.

The Qur'an makes it quite clear that the taking of life unlawfully is prohibited:

"Nor take life – which Allah has made sacred – except for a just cause…" (Al-Qur'an 17:33)

A "just cause" is explained as being in self-defence or as a punishment following the due process of law.

"To those against whom war is made, permission is given to fight, because they are wronged… they are those who have been expelled from their homes in defiance of right… Did not Allah check one set of people by means of another, there would surely have been pulled down monasteries, churches, synagogues and

mosques in which the name of Allah is commemorated in abundant measure…" (Al-Qur'an 22:30-40)

The social context in which "terrorist acts" take place has to be considered before attaching any kind of label. The root causes of community insecurity, oppression or occupation must surely be a factor in reactions to such social conditions. Nelson Mandela once said that the nature of the resistance is determined by the oppressors. International law accepts that people living under illegal military occupation are entitled to fight against the occupiers with whatever means they have at their disposal. If the world does not like, for example, "terrorist suicide bombing" in Palestine (a weapon neither unique to the Palestinians nor invented by them) then, as one Palestinian exile said at a conference in December 2003, "Give us F-16s, Apache helicopters, missiles tanks and heavy weapons, and we'll have a fair fight."

The international laws governing war, formulated in the wake of world war two, were preceded by Islamic law more than 1400 years ago. Very specific guidance is given in the Qur'an and the example of the Prophet (peace be upon him) and his companions. For example:

"Fight in the cause of Allah those who fight you but do not transgress limits, for Allah loves not transgressors. And slay them wherever you catch them, and turn them out from where they have turned you out; for persecution is worse than slaughter. But fight them not at the Sacred Mosque, unless they fight you there [first]; but if they fight you, slay them. Such is the reward of those who reject faith. But if they cease, Allah is Oft-Forgiving, Most Merciful. And fight them on until there is no more persecution and the religion becomes Allah's. But if they cease, let there be no hostility except to those who practise oppression… if then anyone transgresses…against you, transgress you likewise against him. But fear Allah, and know that Allah is with those who restrain themselves." (Al-Qur'an, 2:190-194)

"Fighting is prescribed for you and you dislike it. But it is possible that you dislike a thing which is good for you, and that you love a thing which is bad for you. But Allah knows and you know not." (Al-Qur'an, 2:216)

"…Tumult and oppression are worse than slaughter…" (Al-Qur'an, 2:217)

It is strange, therefore, that Muslims seeking to revive the model Islamic state are branded as "fundamentalists" and "terrorists", and regarded as a threat to world peace.

In all of this, of course, it goes without saying that Muslims may not live up to the ideals of their faith, but that should not be for the want of trying. We are, after all, human beings with human frailties and shortcomings. But we have the ideal example to follow in the life of the Prophet Muhammad (pbuh). That should be our ultimate intention in our worldly dealings, including those with people of other faiths. The Prophet was sent as a "Mercy to mankind"(*Al-Qur'an*, 21:107.), not just to Muslims.

A contemporary Islamic scholar, Sheikh Yusuf Al-Qaradawi, has said, "An extremist seems to address people in this way: 'I have the right to speak, your duty is to listen. I have the right to lead, your duty is to follow. My opinion is right, it cannot be wrong. Your opinion is wrong, it can never be right.' (*Islamic Awakening – between rejection and extremism*, Yusuf Al-Qaradawi, Zain International, 2nd revised edition, 1991, page 33.) This form of "extremism" could be applied to any number of "legitimate" governments and politicians around the world. America's current narrow vision for effectively ruling the world by force is described neatly by Professor Syed Hossein Nasr: "It is... most unfortunate that no present-day power on earth has a perspective wide enough to keep the well-being of the whole earth and its inhabitants in mind." (Syed Hossein Nasr, *Islam and the Plight of Modern Man*, revised edition, Islamic Texts Society, 2002, page 19).

We owe it to ourselves to examine matters more closely before inflaming already fragile situations by linking Islam with terrorism as a matter of course, as if there is no other option to consider. It is neither Islamic to do so, nor indeed particularly Christian. All faiths have actions, events and people to be disowned, and about which we should all seek forgiveness. A more honest and open approach is needed if whole communities are not to be demonised.

Women

O Mankind! Reverence your Guardian Lord...
and the wombs (that bore you)... *{Al-Qur'ān, chapter 4, verse 1}*
Contrary to popular belief, women have a very important role to play in Islāmic society; Muslim women are held in high esteem. This has been made clear by Prophet Muhammad's ﷺ sayings:

A man came to the Prophet ﷺ and said, "Messenger of Allāh, I
desire to go on a military expedition and I have come to

consult you." He ﷺ asked him if he had a mother, and when he replied that he had, he said, "Stay with her, for Paradise is at her feet." {An-Nasā'ī}

A man asked Prophet Muḥammad ﷺ, "O Messenger of Allāh! Who deserves the best care from me?" The Prophet ﷺ said, "Your mother." The man asked, "Who then?" The Prophet ﷺ said, "Your mother." The man asked yet again, "Who then?" Prophet Muḥammad ﷺ said, "Your mother." The man asked once more, "Who then?" The Prophet ﷺ then said, "Your father." {Al-Bukhārī}

"... the best among you is the one who is the best towards his wife." {At-Tirmidhī}

The notion that Muslim women are prisoners in the home, totally subservient to their husbands and fathers and without any rights, is based on ignorance, rather than knowledge, of Islām.

Civilisations have treated women in different ways over the centuries; the advent of Islām established many rights which had previously been denied. In ancient Greece, for example, women were commodities to be bought and sold whilst the Romans regarded women as mere slaves. Until relatively recently in India, Hindu tradition insisted on a widow immolating herself in the flames of her husband's funeral pyre. In pre-Islāmic Arabia, the birth of a female child was not a cause for celebration; baby girls were often buried alive.

It is only within the last 150 years that women have been regarded as citizens in Britain and able to own property, etc. in their own names (not that of their husband). In comparison, Islām granted women the right to earn money and own property independently of their husbands and male relatives over 1400 years ago!

Islām recognises the biological differences between men and women so although they are 'equal', they are not 'the same'. Both are assigned their own roles within society along with the relevant rights and responsibilities. In western society, where the obvious biological differences between men and women are overlooked in the quest for 'equality', the destabilising effect this is having is plain for all to see: broken marriages, illegitimate children and the breakdown of family life can all be said to arise, at least in part, from the move away from and non-acceptance of the supposedly 'traditional' roles for men and women. Combined with sexual 'freedom' as part of women's 'liberation' such liberal attitudes are having a devastating effect on society with corresponding increases in abortions, schoolgirl pregnancies and sexual deviancy.

Women have the right to choose their husbands and should not be forced into marriage against their will. [*see* MARRIAGE] They can also divorce their husband if they so wish; an unsustainable marriage must not take precedence over the happiness of the parties concerned. [*see* DIVORCE] Education is a right for women as well as men and all should have the opportunity to study at the highest levels, the only condition being that their modesty is not put at risk within the study situation. In other words, the Islāmic guidance on dress and the limits on free-mixing with strangers must be observed and preserved. The same applies to the issue of whether women can seek employment or not. Clearly, there are occupations which would make it impossible for the Islāmic codes to be followed and so women should not seek employment in those jobs (for example, as fashion models). The fact that there are relatively few Muslim women in prominent positions in public life should not be used as a judgement against Islām. Instead, we should be asking why the few 'Muslim' ladies employed to present news programmes, for example, should be required to adopt western dress first; would they have been offered such high profile jobs if they were practising their faith and wearing a headcovering?

In their quest for 'equality' some women have degraded themselves, willingly so in many instances, but they have neither gained equality nor liberty. Instead, they have reduced themselves to the status of objects for exploitation by men. A Muslim woman following Islām is under no such male dominated oppression.

> **Verily, the Muslims, men and women,**
> **the believers, men and women,**
> **the men and the women who are obedient (to *Allāh*),**
> **the men and the women who are truthful,**
> **the men and the women who are patient,**
> **the men and the women who are humble,**
> **the men and the women who give charity,**
> **the men and the women who fast,**
> **the men and the women who guard their chastity,**
> **and the men and the women who remember *Allāh* much**
> **with their hearts and tongues;**
> ***Allāh* has prepared for them forgiveness**
> **and a great reward.** *{Al-Qur'ān, chapter 33, verse 35}*

Bibliography

The Holy Qur'ān: text, translation and commentary, 'Abdullah Yusuf 'Ali, Amana Corporation, USA.

Ṣaḥiḥ Al-Bukhārī, English translation by Dr M. Muhsin Khan.

Ṣaḥiḥ Muslim, English translation by 'Abdul Hamid Siddiqui.

Islām: Beliefs and Teachings, Ghulam Sarwar, The Muslim Educational Trust.

What everyone should know about Islām and Muslims, Suzanne Haneef, Kazi Publications, Pakistan.

The Lawful and the Prohibited in Islām (Al-Ḥalāl Wal Ḥarām Fil Islām), Yusuf Al-Qaradawi, American Trust Publications, USA.

The Qur'ān: Basic Teachings, Irving, Ahmad and Ahsan, The Islamic Foundation.

The Islāmic Ruling on Music and Singing, Abu Bilal Mustafa Al-Kanadi, Abul Qasim Bookstore, Saudi Arabia.

Sex Education – The Muslim Perspective, Ghulam Sarwar, The Muslim Educational Trust.

The Laws of Marriage and Divorce in Islām, Abul A'la Mawdudi, translated by Prof Fazl Ahmad, Islamic Book Publishers, Kuwait.

Abortion, Birth Control & Surrogate Parenting – An Islāmic Perspective, Abul Fadl Mohsin Ebrahim, American Trust Publications, USA.

The Miracle of Life, Fatima M. D'Oyen, The Islamic Foundation.

Gender Equity in Islām, Jamal Badawi, American Trust Publications, USA.

The Family Structure in Islām, Hammudah 'Abd al 'Ati, American Trust Publications, USA.

Shari'ah: The Islāmic Law, Abdur Rahman I. Doi, Ta Ha Publishers.

Woman in Islām, Ayesha B. Lemu and Fatima Heren, Islamic Foundation.

The Muslim Woman's Handbook, Huda Khattab, Ta Ha Publishers.

The Muslim Marriage Guide, Ruqaiyyah Waris Maqsood, Quillam Press.

Glossary

ﷺ	Arabic written after the name of the Prophet ﷺ, meaning 'peace and blessings of *Allāh* be upon him'.
Abū Dāwūd	One of the noted compilers of *Ahādīth*, whose main collection is called *Sunan Abū Dāwūd* (d. 888).
Ādam	First human being and first prophet of *Allāh*.
Ahādīth	(Plural of *Hadīth*) Reports of the sayings, deeds and actions approved by Prophet Muhammad ﷺ.
Ahmad	Ahmad ibn Hanbal (d. 875) was one of the noted compilers of *Ahādīth*.
Ākhirah	Life after death. It includes the Day of Judgement and the never-ending life after death.
Al-Bukhārī	One of the noted compilers of *Ahādīth*, whose main collection is called *Sahīh Al-Bukhārī* (d. 870).
An-Nasā'ī	One of the noted compilers of *Ahādīth*, whose main collection is called *Sunan An-Nasā'ī* (d. 915).
At-Tirmidhī	One of the noted compilers of *Ahādīth*, whose main collection is called *Jāmi' At-Tirmidhī* (d. 892).
'Azl	*Coitus interruptus.*
Fiqh	Islāmic jurisprudence – the science of determining the Islāmic ruling on an issue.
Hadd	Punishment prescribed in Islāmic law.
Hadīth	(See *Ahādīth*).
Hajj	The pilgrimage to *Makkah* at the appointed time.
Halāl	That which is lawful (permitted) in Islām.
Harām	That which is unlawful (forbidden) in Islām.
Hudūd	(See *Hadd*).
Ibn Mājah	One of the noted compilers of *Ahādīth*, whose main collection is called *Sunan Ibn Mājah* (d. 886).
'Īd	A day of celebration: *'Īdul Fitr* comes after the end of *Ramadān*, and *'Īdul Adhā* during *Hajj*.
'Iddah	The waiting period during the process of divorce.

Imām Mālik	One of the noted compilers of *Aḥādīth*, whose main collection is called *Al-Muwaṭṭa* (d. 795).
Injīl	The book revealed by *Allāh* to Prophet ʿĪsā (Jesus).
Jahannam	Hell – the place of eternal suffering.
Jannah	Heaven (Paradise) – the place of eternal bliss.
Jihād	Striving to establish Good and remove Evil from society, to gain *Allāh's* pleasure.
Khalīfah	(pl. *Khalāʾifah*) Vicegerent of *Allāh* on the Earth.
Khamr	Intoxicants, especially alcoholic drink and recreational drugs.
Lailatul Qadr	Night of Decrees or Power, a night in the last ten days of the month of *Ramaḍān*.
Maʿāzif	Musical instruments.
Madīnah	The city that Prophet Muḥammad ﷺ emigrated to, where he established the first Islāmic state.
Mahr	Dowry, given by the husband to the wife.
Maḥram	Those relatives to whom marriage is prohibited according to Islāmic law.
Makkah	The place where Prophet Muḥammad ﷺ was born, and the site of the *Kaʿbah*, built by Prophet Ibrāhīm (Abraham) for the worship of *Allāh*. It is the destination for *Ḥajj*.
Makrūh	Something that is not *ḥarām*, but is still disliked.
Mālik	(See *Imām Mālik*).
Muḥammad ﷺ	The final messenger of *Allāh* to mankind (d. 632).
Mujāhid	(pl. *Mujāhidīn*) Someone making *Jihād*.
Muslim	A person who freely and consciously accepts the Islāmic way of life, and sincerely practices it.
	Also, name of one of the noted compilers of *Aḥādīth*, whose main collection is called *Ṣaḥīḥ Muslim*.
Nasāʾī	(See *An-Nasāʾī*).
Qadhf	False accusation.
Qurʾān	This is the sacred book of Muslims, the final book of guidance from *Allāh*, sent down to Muḥammad ﷺ through the angel *Jibrāʾīl*

	(Gabriel) over a period of 23 years.
Ramaḍān	The ninth month of the Islāmic calendar, the month of obligatory fasting.
Ṣalāh	The five compulsory daily prayers, performed in the prescribed manner.
Ṣawm	Fasting during the daylight hours (dawn to sunset) of the month of *Ramaḍān*
Shahādah	The voluntary affirmation that "there is no god but *Allāh* and Muḥammad is the Messenger of *Allāh*".
Sharī'ah	Islāmic law, based on the *Qur'ān* and the *Sunnah*.
Sunnah	The example set by Prophet Muḥammad ﷺ, as recorded in the *Aḥādīth*.
Tashrīq	Three days of celebration after *'Īd ul Aḍḥā*.
Tawrāt	The book revealed by *Allāh* to Prophet Mūsā (Moses).
Tirmidhī	(See *At-Tirmidhī*).
Ummah	Community; in particular, the global Muslim community.
Zabūr	The book revealed by *Allāh* to Prophet Dāwūd (David).
Zakāh	The payment of 2½ percent per annum of one's annual savings to the poor.
Zakātul Fiṭr	Food or equivalent given to the poor by every Muslim at the end of the month of *Ramaḍān* before the prayer of *'Īdul Fiṭr*.
Zinā	Adultery and fornication.

Index

Muslim Educational Trust Publications